speak of it

Speak of it

a memoir

Marcos McPeek Villatoro

University of New Mexico Press
Albuquerque

High Road Books is an imprint of the University of New Mexico Press.

© 2023 by Marcos McPeek Villatoro
All rights reserved. Published 2023
Printed in the United States of America

ISBN 978-0-8263-6532-3 (cloth)
ISBN 978-0-8263-6533-0 (electronic)

Library of Congress Control Number: 2023934616

Founded in 1889, the University of New Mexico sits on the traditional homelands of the Pueblo of Sandia. The original peoples of New Mexico—Pueblo, Navajo, and Apache—since time immemorial have deep connections to the land and have made significant contvwributions to the broader community statewide. We honor the land itself and those who remain stewards of this land throughout the generations and also acknowledge our committed relationship to Indigenous peoples. We gratefully recognize our history.

Cover illustration and lettering by Isaac Morris inspired by Fernando Llort Choussy
Designed by Isaac Morris
Composed in P22 Mackinac, Laca VF

*To my family:
My wife Michelle
and our four children:
Raquel, Emily, David, and Ben.*

Note on the Text

This memoir has been years in the making. It has taken time to reflect upon the story and to write it. Decades have passed since a number of the events occurred. Some of the people in the book have died. Others, I do not know what happened to them, where their own lives took them. I have changed the names of a number of the people in order to respect their privacy.

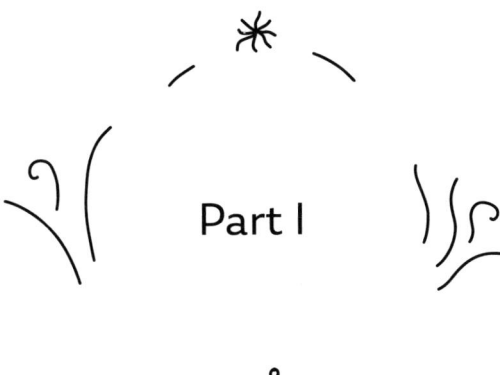

Part I

Chapter 1

Annabelle prayed to CNN every night. She knelt before the television, her clasped hands pressed against her emaciated chest, and mumbled the prayers like a humble monk. She spoke directly to Mary, begging the Mother of God to intercede on her behalf, which meant Annabelle was old-school Catholic. A lock of her long, unkempt gray hair fell over one eye. She didn't brush it away. Every time Anderson Cooper appeared after commercials, Annabelle crossed herself, touching her forehead, abdomen, left then right shoulders with stiff, boney fingers. She looked like she hadn't eaten in days, which might have been the case. She may have been in her early thirties, but seemed older due to the crows' feet wrinkles around her eyes, as though she had squinted under a hot sun most of her life. Her sunken eyes and cheeks showed signs of starvation. I figured she had been living on the streets before they brought her here. Now she was with us in the psych ward, a roof over her head, three square meals a day, a bedroom, and the television. She knelt before it the entire news broadcast. She prayed before other reporters as well, Erin Burnett, Fareed Zakaria, but not with the same fervor. Anderson was her priest, and "AC 360" her mass.

There were other patients in the rec room, women and men who sat silently and stared at a wall or a high window or a piece of furniture. A few roused images from *One Flew Over the Cuckoo's Nest*. One man who looked to be in his thirties, and who had thick, red, frizzy hair, sat on a couch and patted his lap constantly. He mumbled names. Another man, bald, hefty, perhaps in his fifties, paced from one corner of the rec room to the other, all day.

There may have been twenty or thirty patients in the ward, all of us dressed in the purple scrubs of Cedars-Sinai Hospital in Los Angeles. It was a quiet facility, except for the occasional yelps of a young man who sat all day in the cafeteria. When he got a bit too loud, a worker gently calmed him with just a few soft words. This was not Cuckoo's Nest, not at all. No tyrannical, sadistic Nurse Ratched here, no orderlies who ridiculed the patients. But they were strict. In the mornings the nurses at their station handed out our little paper cups of meds with a smile and a straight look. They studied our swallowing to make sure the pills made it down our throats.

A four-inch-wide yellow line ran from one side of the hallway to the other, ten feet from the main entrance. Two orderlies stood in the neutral zone between the line and the swinging doors. I walked a bit too close. "Cuidado," one of the men said, a young Latino who sported a thick, very well-groomed mustache and who looked big enough to tackle an SUV. He held his hands behind his back, like a soldier at ease but still at the ready. He gestured with a nod of his head to the yellow line, smiled at me, and again said in kind Spanish to be careful, and not to take another step.

He was Central American, I could tell by his accent, similar to my mother's Salvadoran tone. I wanted to talk more with him, to keep the Spanish conversation alive. I *craved* it, desperately needed it to help me heal. But he turned to the other orderly, a white man who looked fresh out of college. They spoke in English and ignored me.

Each morning a nurse stood in the rec room and asked us what our goals were for the day. I said that all I wanted to do was rest. She nodded and said that was fine, but I couldn't stay in my room all day, alone, even though there was no lock on the door, nor any object that I could have used. (When I had arrived, they had taken my belt, keys, and shoelaces.) She suggested a therapy group session that focused on one of my two ailments, but she didn't push it.

The food was pretty good, though most of us picked at it and left the plastic plates half-full. Plastic spoons. No forks, no knives. Paper cups for juice, Styrofoam cups for the decaf coffee and herbal teas.

Some of us wandered between the cafeteria, the rec room, and a large patio outside, which the orderlies unlocked twice a day for us to get some sun and have a smoke. They lit our cigarettes and spoke with us as though we were colleagues on a break. I spoke with a patient who was Salvadoran. We chose Spanish, as he struggled with English. I told him my family on my mother's side was from Usulután, a city in the eastern region of El Salvador. The slightest smile broke over his face, as though our connection lifted him out of whatever illness he was suffering. He was a stout man, like a day worker, shorter than I by a few inches, with slightly indigenous features from the Old Country. He said I didn't look *guanaco*—the nickname for Salvadorans—but more Italian, or maybe Argentinian. I told him my father was a gringo. As with the orderly at the front door, I wanted, *needed*, to keep the Spanish going, the language that, for most of my life, had played a fundamental role in my survival. But he just nodded, took a draw from his cigarette, then fell back into his own dark place. One of the orderlies called out in both Spanish and English, "Okay everybody, time to go back in." We obeyed like first graders.

It was a true asylum, a place cut off from all of our worlds. A place of rest, where they had taken away our cell phones. They were strict about visiting hours, knowing that some visitors were at the root of many of our ailments. The orderlies kept vigil over us, watching for a husband or sister or mother to say or do something that would set a patient off. That wasn't my issue. My wife, Michelle, who had helped me through the days before the breakdown, could do only so much. She and I sat at a small, round table. It confused her, how I smiled and asked how our four kids were doing. She said they were fine, but both of us knew they weren't. They had seen too much.

Michelle was afraid. This was my first trip to a psych ward. I wanted to believe that my time there would be a respite for my family. But this seventy-two-hour hold, for them, was as bad as all the howling at home. This time, I had lost all control: at one point, I had dropped to my knees and bashed my head against our kitchen's tile floor, over and over again. I needed constant surveillance, something my family couldn't do on their own.

I needed no self-control at Cedars-Sinai. The staff did all the controlling. Along with my regular medications—two antipsychotics and one antidepressant—they dosed me with a little something extra to lessen the mania. Something soporific, but not too much. The breakdown still pulsed in me. I couldn't read, couldn't write, and had a hard time watching the news with praying Annabelle. But I wasn't screaming or running my head into a door or cutting myself. The seclusion of the ward, along with its rules and burly orderlies, kept me in check. The rules freed me. The monastic seal of the front door, and its yellow line drawn on the floor, kept the world from coming in. The new medication let me rest. I slept for the first time in five days.

*

Something had set me off, had unleashed the two diseases in me. Something that felt cosmic, a lining up of the stars. A form of dark fate, or a mean game of chance among the gods. I don't believe that anymore. But sometimes, due to the way it went down, I have wondered if someone had intentionally set it up to try to break me, to get me to commit suicide—I wonder if *he* somehow made it happen. But that's giving him too much credit.

I ended up in Cedars-Sinai because of the Internet. I had forgotten to renew my website, "marcosvillatoro.com," where my books were listed. A pornography ring had bought it and stuck a porn site onto my page. It stripped out all of my writings and biography. It wasn't just a general porn site, but one that hawked incest-rape videos.

It was a cheaply constructed site, with ostentatious photos of naked, supposed family members interlocked in violent sexual acts. There were buttons to click that took the visitor to the credit card page. Underneath the pictures, the wild-font captions clarified: "Brother-Sister Fucking! Father-Daughter dick-suck! Son-Mother pussy-eat!" Whoever had built the site struggled with English; at the bottom, they'd written in tiny letters, "All are these, actors."

A computer engineer friend figured out that the buyers of my name were from St. Petersburg, Russia. One of my books had recently been translated into Russian. Perhaps the pornographers thought my name got ample traffic and that from among those who checked out my work, the site would grab the attention of a few perverts. But how did they know of my past? How was it that their site sold the thing so specific to my life?

A week after first seeing the web page, I broke the rim of a ceramic coffee cup against the edge of my desk, took a large shard of it, jabbed it into my forearm and raked the skin toward my wrist, as though to connect the new cuts with an old scar. I slashed the other arm, my bicep and right thigh. Michelle and my two middle-school sons found me shriveled up on the floor, blood stains on the wood, my clothes, and smeared over my skin. Even in the moment of the episode, I could see the horror in my sons' eyes. Michelle leaned over me and touched my shoulder. I bellowed. It was too much for us all. The porn site had gone beyond the beyonds.

*

I've never been able to fully understand my relative's actions. I have, however, always remembered. He lived with us through the years of my childhood. I can still see what he did to me; how could I not? It happened several times, for over a year; it seared the moment into my brain and left a permanent brand there. He, a teenager, had me, five, take my clothes off, then he'd take off his, all in the silence of a house with no adults present. He whispered calmly, made me lie on his bed and told me not to move. He made my tiny body quake with things that a five-year-old ought not to feel: confusion, horror, and arousal. I stared over his shoulder to the right, upper corner of the room until it was over. When he finished, we dressed in silence, except for his *Now, don't tell anybody, or you'll get in trouble.*

All of the rapes, repetitive, near-liturgical, come together into one. And they did happen as I remember. I know this because thirty years later he called, screaming for forgiveness. It seemed out of the blue, but something had triggered him off: A poem.

He said he had been meandering through a Barnes & Noble Bookstore in Knoxville, Tennessee, and found my book of poetry. I can imagine him, not meandering at all, but heading straight to the bookshelf where he might find my work. I knew full-well what he was seeking out: Had I written about it? I had, in four short lines of a poem that was tucked way in the back of the collection.

> No tainted memory of shame,
> Though the children still play games
> Taught by naked kin
> Who hide in shadows.

He had been "thumbing through" the book (I imagine him testing it for bombs) when he came across those four lines. They were too much for him. He bolted out of the bookstore.

Over the phone, he spoke in a wail of a confession, about how what he had done had haunted him, and he was sorry, terribly sorry for it all. It was messy. He wept, hiccupped, blew his nose. It lasted a while. Four lines of a poem had broken him. In that breaking, I made a decision, for what reason, I'm not sure, though I'm glad I did.

I asked him for specifics, which I chronicled in my journal while he confessed. Yes, it had gone on for over a year. Yes, it happened at night, when my mother and father slept in alcohol-soaked dreams. I asked him why he suddenly quit doing it. He said, "Because you yelled." The last time, he told me, happened at night. I was asleep. He was trying to take me from behind. According to him, I screamed "Quit it! It hurts!" and didn't stop yelling until he slipped out of my bed and rushed to his bedroom. Even with alcohol running through our parents' brains, he knew they might wake up. This is the greatest gift the relative has given me, a memory that I don't recall: I yelled. I was angry. Because of his confession, I saw that the anger had been with me since that first yelp.

He explained how he had suffered the anguish for what he had done, the guilt that had haunted him all his life. I didn't console him, but kept writing the notes in my journal, thinking that, someday, I might use them.

Then he blurted out his reasons for calling: to apologize, to ask for forgiveness, and—the hook—to beg me not to ever write about what he had done. It was all an echo of the past, *Don't tell anyone*. And I, programmed at age five to abide, told him, as an adult, that I wouldn't. I have obeyed. Until now.

*

Writing has been a way to make a semblance of sense out of the chaos. You'll find shadowy allusions to the trauma and mental illness throughout my work. But it is in my journals where I've written about them head-on. Forty-seven years of journal writing. Over fifty tomes, which are all shapes and sizes, most of them black Moleskines. Around fourteen thousand pages in all. Keeping a constant diary, for me, is beyond obsession; it's a way to survive. There are the regular entries about high school, college, my wife, children, jobs, and all my notes on whatever writing project I was working on at the time. But they are also pockmarked with the constant, decades-old question, *What is happening to my mind?*

The handwriting changes, depending on the moods. During the calm times, it's fairly smooth and easy to read. Then there are the erratic entries that make the words undecipherable—scrawls of sentences that expand and contract, that don't follow the lined notebooks, words that scatter over the page as though a small explosive had blown them apart. These were written when the past became too much, or when the meds weren't working, or something, anything, set me off. Fear and rage swamp the pages. When the mania hits, the sentences stretch long and are comma-less, as though I'm trying to compete with Faulkner. When the depression sets in, the sentences shorten, become stumps of burdened thoughts.

Then there are all the entries regarding my blood lines, the fact that I am from two cultures, Salvadoran and Appalachian. It's a strange mix, I know. The writings about the two ethnicities aren't born in a vacuum. They are interwoven with the trauma and the fight to keep my mind in a certain equilibrium. They are a tool in my survival kit. What does it mean to be bicultural? This, for me, isn't simply an intellectual question. It's a rumination that pumps through the marrow of who I am.

According to the journals, I have had episodic breakdowns throughout the decades, since my teenage years, when the other illness first raised its head. I have bipolar disease. It runs in my Villatoro family. Sometimes I wonder if, had it not been for the abuse in childhood, the manic depression wouldn't be so "dramatic." New studies bring this to light: according to the *International Journal of Bipolar Disorders*, childhood traumatic events are risk factors for developing manic depression. A study at the University of Manchester found that people who are manic depressive are three times as likely as the general population to have suffered emotional, physical, or sexual abuse as children.

Bipolar is genetic. Rape is diabolical. When they work in tandem, I go mad. One sets off the other. Stress ignites the bipolar; a portal opens to the past; childhood swamps me. Or the childhood rushes me from out of nowhere, like a stiletto through my skull, and unleashes the madness.

The journals take me inward, allow me to explore the connections between trauma, mental illness, and heritage. Those personal writings have helped me make certain decisions, such as the choosing of one culture over the other. Again, a way to survive.

*

I didn't want to leave the hospital. It was safe there. For three days I wandered in a neutral zone, along with others who were suffering their own mental struggles. There was a strange comfort about that, the fact that I was not alone in the world. Some looked like they were in far worse shape than I was. Others were more lucid and able to carry on a conversation for a while.

I sat with one young man in the cafeteria. He might have been in his early twenties. We talked about our families. His wasn't at the root of his illness. He was schizophrenic, which surprised me, the way he articulated his thoughts so clearly. He had been in the hospital for a number of weeks, which had allowed for his new meds to set in. He had his parents to thank for putting him in here. I didn't tell him about the trauma in my childhood, nor the website, but spoke about the bipolar as though it were my only problem. It felt safer that way.

We talked about our medications. He took a number of pills each day. One of them was an antipsychotic that I also used. But he rattled off the names of the others, ones I had never heard of before. "As long as I stay on them, I'm okay. But sometimes, well, I quit taking them. That's when all hell breaks loose in my head."

He didn't explain why he would get off the meds. I figured it was because, when taking them, he felt better, and maybe figured he wasn't sick anymore. But this long stretch in the psych ward showed him how he had to stay on them in order to survive.

When he said that, I shook. I had been on medications for years, and they had overall done their job. I still had mood swings, but they weren't anything like the dramatic highs and depthless holes that I had suffered since high school. The recent years had been a respite from all that. Like my schizophrenic acquaintance, taking the pills daily kept me sane.

Then the website hit. It was too, too much. No amount of pharmaceuticals could pull me out of the chaos. It was as though the site had bashed through a wall that I had spent all my life constructing. Pills, therapy, relationships, exercise, sleep, writing, all were shattered by what had come out of St. Petersburg. The only thing left was my Latino heritage, but it too suffered the blow.

The seventy-two-hour hold was up. I had to meet with a couple of psychiatrists, who checked me to see if I was ready to go home. They asked me questions: Did I feel any better than how I did before coming to Cedars-Sinai? Did I think I was a danger to myself or to others? Was I suicidal? The cuts on my arms, covered over with gauze and tape—would that happen again? Was I ready to return to my family? Would they be supportive? And would I stay on my medications?

My family. That's when it hit me—I didn't want to stay any longer in the hospital. I was missing them terribly. I worried for them, knowing that all that had happened had also beaten against them like a thousand hammers. My sons, who had witnessed the breakdown; my college-age daughters, who had not been there, but who knew. And my wife, *Ay, Michelle, Mi Vida.* That was my nickname for her: she was My Life.

So, I lied to the psychiatrists. No, I wasn't suicidal. The cuts were a one-time thing and would not happen again. I felt better now than when I first came to the ward.

The only thing I didn't lie about was my family. I needed them. I wanted to assure them that everything was going to be okay, that the time in the hospital had shaken the horror out of me. We would gather once again around the supper table and enjoy not just the meal, but the *sobremesa*, the table-talk that many times lasted for over an hour. We would get back on track, and return to our prehospital lives as though all this was a mere blip. All lies, not to the doctors, but to myself.

They signed the release papers. I rushed to my room to pack. Michelle would pick me up in a couple of hours. It felt like a semblance of happiness. Then I looked at myself in the bathroom's steel mirror. I could see it; how was it the doctors had missed it? Those were my eyes, but no, they were not—somebody else had replaced me, someone hollow.

An orderly had me sit in a wheelchair. He took me out of the ward and to the front lobby. Michelle was waiting for me. I stood up, thanked the orderly, then turned to her. She looked at me and I could see it, can see it still: the godawful fear of those who have witnessed too much. We hugged. I held her tight, as though to save her from myself. "I'm okay," I said. "I'll be all right."

All my children were home to greet me. I lied to them with a smile and gentle words, promising them that I would be okay. I would dig out of this hole, as I had done so many times in my life. It just took all the tricks to do it, all the tools that I had gathered throughout the years to take care of myself.

I wouldn't be all right. The website would remain in the public domain for over a year. All that time, my name was tied to incest rape, for all the world to see. I rattled through the days. Somehow, I returned to work at the university. Teaching kept me busy, but as soon as the classes were over, I rushed to my car and drove home, barely able to see the 405 freeway due to all the tears. Sometimes I screamed.

I had been working on a novel at the time but abandoned it after the hospital stay. But there were the journals, all stacked up in a corner of my room. I sat in the recliner and stared at them. I couldn't move. It wasn't just depression; it was the horror. And sitting alone in a room was not a good idea. For I *was* a danger to myself. A few days after leaving the hospital, I took a cutlery knife to my upper legs, small nicks, just enough to shunt the fear in my head to the pain over my skin.

Finally, I turned to the latest journal and started writing. It was like trying to shovel through hot coals. I wrote about what had happened, but even putting down the word *website* was enough to tip me over the edge. This was not right; the journals, all my life, had been a place of refuge, where I could put down my perturbed thoughts. But now my hand shook. The world was caving in.

I write both in English and Spanish in the journals, switching from one to the other every so many months. In the days of the website, I happened to be writing in English. After the hospital stay, I turned to Spanish. It seemed like a desperate act, a way of escaping—I could hide in my mother's language.

Inevitably, the writings turned to childhood, but not only to the trauma. There was more to me than just incest and mental illness. I was forcing myself to believe this, pushing myself to see the other aspects of my life. I had to take the journey again, had to pick up the broken pieces and try to put them back together. It was exhausting, and it didn't cure me. But it helped me see how the world had shaped me, and how I had shaped myself.

Chapter 2

I was strange and everyone knew it, but Blake Putnam sang about it. It was 1973. He and I were eleven and listening to Cher's song "Half-Breed," which had gone gold that year. The way Cher sang, you'd believe her to be a pissed-off Cherokee. Blake and I sang with her, hurling the words across the living room.

> *Half-Breed! That's all I ever heard...*
> *Both sides were against me since the day I was born!*

Somewhere in the chorus Blake stopped, looked at me, and had an epiphany. "Hey," he said, "that's what you are, a half-breed!"

Blake was my best friend. We'd grown up together since the tricycle years. He wasn't insulting me. I don't doubt there might have been a little jealousy to his statement, that I had something special about me, a thing that Cher, with her throaty, voracious singing, celebrated. We figured she was a half-breed too, from a short film we saw of her during the Sonny and Cher show. She was sitting on a black horse, dressed as a sexy squaw, with a white cutoff top that enhanced her cleavage. Her skin was my El Salvadoran mother's color. We didn't know that was body makeup.

I hadn't been called a half-breed until that day. But something was in the air and always had been. My family was different from all the white families in our neighborhood—a completely white neighborhood. I knew this, but couldn't articulate it. But Blake did, and he did it in praise of who, or what, I was.

We were in my father's world of Appalachia. Rogersville was a small town, around forty-five hundred souls, mostly white, with a small and rather hidden African American population. As far as we knew, my mother was the only Latin American in the region.

We had an old shoebox of photos from the years that had passed long before I came along. As a kid, I'd pull the box out of the closet and study the deckle-edged pictures of my parents' honeymoon days, especially the ones of them traveling on a 1947 Harley Davidson Knucklehead motorcycle, and try to imagine their lives. What was it like for a white Appalachian man and a Salvadoran woman to ride across America in 1947? How were they accepted by each other's families? How did they survive the laws of US racism? In the pictures, they look like they didn't give a damn.

World War II had brought them together. In 1942 my father, Ralph McPeek, had joined the Navy and served in the South Pacific. Two years later Mamá Amanda and her family immigrated to the United States from El Salvador. The Villatoros moved to San Francisco, where my mother got a job in a sewing factory. She washed blood off Navy life jackets and sewed closed the bullet holes. The jackets were then sent back to the ships in the Pacific theater.

After the war, Dad was discharged in San Francisco. They first saw each other in a coffee shop. Dad was peeking over the edge of the *San Francisco Chronicle* and giving her glances. "¡Ay, esos ojos tan verdes!" Mamá told me when I was a kid—he had green eyes, the color of fecundity in the Old Country. He introduced himself. They had coffee together. Dad didn't speak a lick of Spanish. Mamá had studied English, but couldn't understand Dad's Appalachian voice, with its elongated words and drawn-out syntax. Within the year, they married.

Dad put her on the back of the Harley and took her to his family in Tennessee. It was the first of five road trips across the United States on the motorcycle. They wore leather all over: chaps, jackets, gloves, even their helmets that hugged their heads tight. They wore goggles and black riding boots. They followed their whims: my mother would miss my grandmother, who lived in San Francisco's Mission District, so they'd ride back. Dad would get a construction or mechanic job in Tennessee. They mounted the bike and returned to the Appalachian Mountains. They didn't take the direct way, but meandered north and south, into Minnesota and Texas. Five cross-country trips on a motorcycle, with a couple of treks to the races in Daytona. By the time I was sixteen, the photos and their stories were a bit too much to handle. It hurts a teenager to know that his parents were bigger bad-asses than he will ever be.

They might have been too blind with love in the beginning to worry about any racial concerns, but in Tennessee, they got a heaping dose of it. My McPeek grandparents couldn't make heads or tails out of who (or what) my mother was. She wasn't black but she sure as hell wasn't white. They'd never heard of El Salvador. They believed their son had blemished the family, and they worried about grandchildren in a world where laws against miscegenation still dwelled in the southern mind.

After all those trips between California and Tennessee, they wrecked just outside of Knoxville. Three years of riding over twenty thousand miles, and a small patch of gravel ended it. The Harley slung them off and skidded on its side over the shoulder. The dump onto the highway was enough to shake the wildness out of them. They patched up the cuts where the road had torn through the leather and jeans and rode back into Appalachia, where Dad sold the motorcycle, bought a very used Chevy, and built a house in a small neighborhood. They didn't get down to miscegenating until well into their marriage.

We were living in San Francisco when I was born. (The Harley wreck hadn't quelled all their wanderlust. We just made the trips by car.) I was born in the Mission District and that pleases me. It legitimizes me. For my home city was an outpost of El Salvador.

I remember when my abuelita—my grandmother—once took me by the hand, and we walked through the Mission to buy groceries. Two young, colorfully dressed Latina women were standing at the corner, talking and looking up and down the street. Abuelita called out to them, and we stopped to have a chat. My mother, years later, told me that the prostitutes rented a room in Abuelita's house and always paid on time. The two women cooed at me, called me all the things a Salvadoran woman calls a little boy, *¡Ay mi corazón, rey de mi vida!* They bent down and kissed me on the cheeks, leaving lipstick on both sides of my face.

I lived my first four years in the Mission. I have memories from there, enough to keep my love for the barrio alive. My mother, when I was in my teens and longing for my *latinidad*, helped fill the gaps between my own recollections. She told me stories about the relatives, the people who lived in the house, the times she and her mother made tamales together. I peppered her with questions about those days. She was more than happy to share. She basked in the fact that her teenage son was looking for his roots.

My own sensory memories burn deep. I saw, smelled, heard the world that I had been born into. It was a Latin American barrio of Mexicans, Guatemalans, Nicaraguans, Hondurans, and, in my grandmother's three-story Victorian house on Capp Street, Salvadorans. According to Mamá, Abuelita had bought the home three years after leaving El Salvador. She had paid it off by renting all the rooms. There was a constant hustle and bustle of people living under the same roof. The renters sometimes crowded into the parlor, put on records and danced till way past midnight, undulating their hips and swinging one another around the room. And oh how the women loved me! I was the *gringo-guanaco* child, a special mix of Salvadoran and white blood. According to them, I had the best of both worlds. And I spoke Spanish. Abuelita insisted on talking with me in her native tongue (*our* native tongue), and the other women followed suit, including my mother.

San Francisco was the Salvadoran diaspora that fed me all things guanaco. I still hold on to that, though, except for the first few years of life, I've not lived there. But it was and still is my Salvadoran Emerald City, a place of the other language, a world of brown people who coddled the off-white newborn son.

San Francisco was loud and frisky, with Spanish spoken up and down Mission Street, and vendors hawking tortillas and tacos on every corner. There was music: Manny Chavez, Carlos Gardel, Ritchie Valens, all tumbled out of kitchen windows and passing cars. And the odors: every shape and form of cooked corn you can imagine, along with the heat and smell of rice and beans. In these memories, my father is missing. He worked at a gas station all day, and at night tended to stay out of the loud, Spanish-speaking crowd.

Then we moved to Tennessee. We were suddenly three thousand miles away from the voices and communal protection of the Salvadoran women. Tennessee, where the second childhood began and tried to kill off the first one. In Appalachia, Dad said to Mamá, as if he had spoken for the first time after the San Francisco years, "Never talk to this boy except in English. No more goddamn Spanish, not here, not in *this* house."

Dad's moratorium on Spanish hurt Mamá, but it didn't surprise her. He was Appalachian to the bone, and even though he had married outside his race, he lived a southern white man's ways. Maybe he did so to protect me. Cutting his boy off from the other heritage may have been a way for me to be accepted by the locals. Or maybe he had simply felt left out in San Francisco, with everyone talking Spanish. But according to Mamá, he had turned against her native language as though having thought about it for a long while. My mother has never been one to cower. Dad tried to slam the door on San Francisco, but he couldn't strip his wife of her culture. She couldn't talk to her son in Spanish. But she had other strategies.

Although we lived in a deep corner of a monolingual region, in the hermetically sealed Appalachian Mountains, Mamá, as much as she could, sowed her El Salvadoran customs in the Latino-parched land of Tennessee. The pulse of her small country ran through the house. We ate rice, black beans, tortillas, tamales, and pupusas (my abuelita mailed sacks of cornmeal flour to us, something you couldn't find in the local grocery stores). Mamá decorated the entire house with artifacts from the Central American countries: gourds, maracas, a painting of campesinos working on a coffee plantation, a fishing net that covered an entire wall, like a gigantic blue and white web. And we danced, she and I, an act that, in an evangelical world, made us minions of Satan. She taught me how to move my hips just as the folks did in the Mission—undulations of movement, like liquid. Mamá had the old records from San Francisco. She sang in Spanish. When Dad wasn't around, she cooed at me Salvadoran phrases, *Vení mi corazón*, as she had me climb her lap for a sudden hug. She talked with my grandmother on the phone every Saturday. Through these acts of trickery, I heard the forbidden language.

My mother's dancing and Salvadoran cooking must have blinded me to what she saw beyond the walls of our house. When I turned six, she had to send me out into that world, and dreaded doing so. I didn't know how painful this was to her, until, at age ninety, after my father died, she moved in with my family and me. We were drinking coffee together and talking, in Spanish, about those old days. "I was so scared," she said, "the first day I took you to school."

"Why?"

She seemed surprised that I asked, and looked at me as though I were a little dense. "Because of the way I knew they were going to treat you."

Over that coffee, she told me how people had thought about us, the mixed-race family with a mother who came from Way Out There. When she first had gone to east Tennessee, people had stared at her wherever she went. She felt their hardened eyes. Once, at a restaurant, while Mamá and Dad were eating supper, a woman sitting at a nearby booth scowled at them. Not everyone was like this. Many greeted them with a smile and a handshake. One fellow, a teacher named Mr. Cunningham, liked to practice Spanish with Mamá. There were, she said to me, good people around them. But the malicious stares and whispers singed her. She worried for me, knowing that once I was in the school system, the southern world would get to work setting the record straight.

She was right. It was Hazel Walker who broke the racial ice. It happened early on, in the first days of first grade. Hazel wasn't one to mince words. She looked at me over the short table in the classroom and said, "My daddy says you'll never go to college."

I had no idea what college was, so I said, "Okay."

But she wasn't finished. Because of my background, I probably wouldn't make it through high school. My dad, according to Mr. and Mrs. Walker, was poor white trash who had been born in a sharecropper's shack in the middle of a tobacco crop. My mother was a foreigner. "That means you won't go to college."

It didn't occur to me that I was worthy of such table talk, especially in the Walker home. Their station in life was far above ours. Mr. Walker was the owner of the local Chevrolet dealership and a city councilman. My father, a mechanic, was unemployed much of the time. He also struggled with alcohol and depression, especially when he had no job. Mamá had to work in order to cover the bills.

Hazel's parents were right. My father *had* been born in a sharecropper shack and lived his childhood and adolescent years in a tobacco crop. He had a fifth-grade education. He was, in the Walkers' minds, the essence of poor white trash.

When I was in fourth grade, Dad landed a job as a school bus driver. I remember feeling some pride about that. It was a thrill, when I boarded, to see him in in the driver's seat. "Morning, son," he'd say to me in his gravelly voice.

The pride ended the day Hazel and her best friend, Bethany Callahan, sat in the bus seat opposite mine. They didn't need to raise their voices, but they did, and they parroted what they had heard at home. Had their parents also taught them how to sneer? No longer did they refer to their mothers and fathers, no "My daddy says . . ." They spoke on their own accord. They owned the words. "I'll be surprised if we get to school alive," one of them said, followed by the other's, "I don't doubt he took a couple shots of whiskey the moment he woke up."

I turned my head slightly toward them. They were smiling and looking ahead through the windshield. They kept talking about my father. I turned and stared out the side window and tried my best not to cry. Then they tired of the subject and slipped into fourth grade again, talking about a new doll, a mean older sister, and what they hoped to get for Christmas.

They weren't the only ones sizing me and my family up. One day a group of boys approached me on the playground. They weren't bullies; I suppose they were just racially curious. We talked for a bit, something about one of our teachers. Or maybe we were talking about girls. I don't know; I just remember Frank Callahan suddenly asking me, "What's your mom?"

I wasn't sure how to answer that. He clarified, "I mean, she's different from anybody around here."

I said that she was Salvadoran. One of the others asked, "What's that?" I stumbled through some words, and ended up saying that it was like being Mexican. They turned to each other, suddenly ignoring me, and got to work figuring out this racial problem. Dark mother, white father. Then it dawned on them. Frank turned back to me. "So, that makes you a mongrel." He said it in the same tone as "Pass the salt."

I remember those racist, classist moments, but they don't compare with the memories of what was happening at home, and inside me. There was much more going on in my brain in those first years of school. The relative had stopped hurting me when I was six. The ramifications of the abuse were just beginning. My stomach turned against me. The pain was so excruciating, I bent over from it. Diarrhea plagued me. One afternoon in first grade, I was playing on the slide in the school yard. I couldn't control it. It spewed out of me, and ran down the metal slide, just as I pushed myself down. I was wearing shorts. I slid down the slick of shit. A girl said, "Oh gosh, he poo-pooed!" Somebody must have told Mrs. Goins, who was keeping watch over us. She was so kind. She put her hand on my shoulder and shepherded me to the building. She called my mother to bring me a new set of clothes. I don't remember Mamá showing up. She might have dropped them off and rushed back to work. In the school bathroom, Mrs. Goins cleaned me, helped me into the underwear and pants and socks then took the soiled clothes away.

Chapter 3

There was a word that my mother used a lot while talking with Abuelita over the phone, *púchica*. When I was a kid, I asked her what it meant. She laughed, "Oh, it's like, 'wow,' or 'gosh.' It's whenever you're surprised by something."

I liked the word, and tried it out at school. A long black snake had made its way onto the playground. Girls screamed. Boys tried to pick it up. I said, "Púchica, that is one big snake." Someone asked what that meant. I gave the definition, thinking they'd be impressed. They weren't. They just thought it was weird.

I started to lose the meaning of the Spanish words I had learned in San Francisco. The sound of the language, its rhythm, didn't escape me. Still, the separation was happening. Something was being lost, no matter how much Mamá threw hooks of memory between the El Salvador of the Mission District and east Tennessee. I didn't say púchica anymore. My accent turned Appalachian. It was the inevitable assimilation that a kid goes through whenever pulled out of one culture and put into another—you become one with the new world. The culture of my first years in San Francisco dissipated. I was forgetting. My grandmother, my aunts and uncles, the dances, the raucous parties—we had left that all behind.

Then, when I was seven, my parents made a decision, one that, given my father's moratorium on Spanish, made no sense at all: to move to El Salvador. It was a spontaneous and desperate idea. They had suffered months of unemployment in Tennessee. Mamá sold Dad the idea with job opportunities: In El Salvador, she could be a translator—for whom she didn't say—and Dad a mechanic or manager of a small farm. They scraped up money for plane tickets. We spent the summer in El Salvador, to check out the possibilities of living there, as well as visit family in Mamá's hometown of Usulután.

I was afraid. Three years had passed since we'd left California, and for a child, three years might as well be three decades. But after the first week or so, I started to like it. El Salvador didn't look like the Mission District, but it had what I needed: the women. They were a little quieter than those in my grandmother's house, but they still coddled me with their sudden embraces.

San Francisco had been my garden of Latino delights. El Salvador was the root. The smells of roasted meats, tamales, and refried black beans, soaked the air inside my great-grandmother's adobe house. The images, sounds, and odors flood me now: the emaciated cows, the hourly ringing of an old tin bell in the church tower, the men who left their houses at dawn to work in the corn fields, with their machetes that hung from their rope belts. The bleating goats, the scampering chickens, the roosters that belted out their *¡Ki-kiri-kiris!* (Spanish for *cock-a-doodle-doo!*) whenever they wanted, even at noon. The women who, after working since four in the morning making tortillas, took breaks to sit with their neighbors to gossip. The ruthless heat. The sudden rains that thickened the humidity. The Spanish was strange and recognizable at the same time, a mirror of sound that reflected the cooing and laughter of the women in San Francisco.

I remember the black and red train that took us from the capital of San Salvador to Mamá's hometown. It looked like a locomotive from the nineteenth century, and it hauled us through the mountains and valleys with its *CLACK CLACK CLACK* and the acrid, black smoke that billowed from the stack. A goat sat next to me in the aisle. Poor farmers carried their animals on the train, chickens, a pig, and that goat. I had drunk a thick, red soda that was more sugar than liquid. It didn't go down well. I vomited the soda onto the goat's head. It looked at me with glassy eyes while licking the sugar-thick beverage from its chops.

Everyone was dark like Mamá. A whole country of brown people. We were so far from my father's world. In El Salvador, I was timid, after having lived in a monolingual land for three years. But the maternal love of the country calmed me. Women loved me without knowing me, except through the pictures my grandmother had shown them.

Children ran everywhere. Some of them were my cousins. I don't recollect any of their names. They looked at me like the kids did in Tennessee.

I was some strange thing that they were trying to figure out. I didn't speak Spanish. I had light skin. I'm sure, in their eyes, I looked much more like my father than Mamá.

They weren't shy about their curiosity. They talked to me as though I would at some point break out of stupidity and start speaking with them. It was too much. I ran to my mother, who was chatting with my great-grandmother Martina in the kitchen. The kids stopped at the door. They still bantered with one another, only more quietly, but not quietly enough for Martina. She snapped at them. They took off.

They wouldn't leave me alone. They weren't mean about it, they just followed me around. I wanted to escape. One afternoon, I hid in a hammock, tucking myself into its belly and pulling the edges over me, like a cocoon. It didn't work. The kids crowded around the hammock. A girl peeled it open. All those sets of eyes looking down at the gringo kid—it was unnerving.

A boy on the dirt street called out to them. They ran off and joined him.

I looked over the hammock's edge and out the door. They squatted together in a circle and looked down at the ground. A game of marbles. The boy who had called out to them took his turn. I got out of the hammock, walked to the door, half-hiding myself behind the frame.

The girl who had opened the hammock looked my way. Without any hesitation, she called out to me. I didn't move. She left the circle and approached me. She spoke. I looked at her then looked away. She made a motion with her arm to follow her, back to the circle where the kids were playing marbles. She made room for me, telling the others to move over, to give me a place to squat.

I didn't know how to play. They flicked the balls with precision, knocking one marble after another out of the circle. The girl gave me a turn. She was very pretty; she looked like she could have been my mother's daughter. She showed me how to flick a ball. I did. The marble went flying through the air, over one boy's shoulder. They all laughed, then the girl hushed them. She retrieved the marble and motioned for me to do it again.

At night they played a game called "Kill the bats." That's exactly what it was. It was simple: stand out on the dirt road with a long stick in hand and wait for the bats to fly by. Some kids used wide boards like paddles. All of them had their weapons at the ready. They stared at the sky, waiting.

23

I didn't want to play. I imagined a bat falling and biting me on the neck on the way down. The kids flung their sticks and boards over their heads. No luck for a while, until one of them popped one out of the sky. Then another and another. Over a dozen bats lay on the dirt road. The kids who had hit them collected the animals. It was simple—who could kill the most?

The girl had killed two. She brought them to me, holding them upside down by their legs. One was bloody from the blow. I didn't understand. Did she want to give them to me, or did she just want to show me her yield? It must have been the latter, because, after a few seconds, she ran off and joined the other children.

After a few weeks, I wasn't so strange to them. They treated me like just another kid on the block. We went swimming in a nearby river, played soccer on the street, and sometimes ate together in my great-grandmother's home. It was a good time. Still, I felt on the edge of their group. It was the language; I could not speak. I had no voice here. Some of the words were coming back, the ones I had grown up with in San Francisco. Now I know that, if we had stayed, if my parents had found jobs, I would have picked up the Spanish quickly. I would have assimilated back into the culture of my first years of life.

Unfortunately, a war broke out while we were there, "The Soccer War" between El Salvador and Honduras, over land issues at the border. "I'll burn in hell before I live in this fucking country," Dad said, or something to that effect. We returned to Tennessee. Now, I see that summer as an early touchstone of my survival, one as powerful as the words I had screamed at the relative just a year before, *Quit it! It hurts!* That season in Central America, I believe, is when the longing for my Salvadoran culture set in, and though it submerged once again when we returned to the United States, it would bubble up years later.

After the trip, and back in Tennessee, I got down to being Appalachian again. None of this was a conscious effort, it just happened, naturally—again, the need for a child to fit in. The desire to break out of the white, monolingual world wouldn't happen until many years later, when I would move to Central America, where I would live years in the same land that, in the summer of '69, had loved me without knowing me.

Chapter 4

In Tennessee, school was a refuge from what was going on in our house. I look fondly back on my grade school years. Yes, I remember meanness, and it wasn't all directed at me. There were bullies and cliques. Older kids pulled harsh tricks on the younger students. My friend Blake, who was a bit smaller than most of us, suffered their shenanigans. I remember him crossing over the monkey bars when a cadre of seventh graders came up from behind and pulled his shorts down, underwear and all.

But the classroom was calm. Some teachers had to come down hard on a few of the tough kids, but this was a small town, where most of the marms were related to the students—an aunt who taught fifth grade, a mother who taught eighth, an older sister who was more than happy to come down on her little brother. Those blood relations kept a certain respect alive, or it might have been fear—with that network of kin, few kids acted up.

Mrs. Romans was our eighth-grade English teacher, and she knew all the tricks. She was a little thing, just slightly shorter than most of us. Her face looked like a sun-dried apple. Her hair was frizzy and gray, and her arms and legs were as skinny as sticks. But as old as she was (she could have been our grandmother, or maybe our great-grandmother), she had the energy of a much younger teacher.

She taught us English literature and grammar, but there was more to it. She would sometimes tell us a story from her younger days, such as when she fell in love in fifth grade with Randy Marshall, who, ten years later, ended up marrying her sister.

Ours was an old brick school with two floors, and had been built in the late 1800s. Mrs. Romans pointed out the area of the room where she herself had sat God knows how many decades before us. I pictured her as a twelve-year-old, wrinkled-up student, sitting amongst us. Then, after so much storytelling, she'd reel us in, "All right, let's get back to Huck and Jim. Where'd we leave off?"

She had us read aloud. This was hard on some, easier on others. Whenever Bill Weaver got picked, I cringed; he was a shy student and trembled when he read. As he stumbled along, Mrs. Romans sat quietly, patiently, on her stool, sometimes helping him with a word or two. "Very good, Bill," she'd say, and ask another student to pick up where Bill had left off. Joy Paxton could read better than any of us, but she received the same, equal compliment, "Very good, Joy."

After calling on a few more of us to read, she'd say, "All right, it's my turn." That mellifluous, soft, Appalachian tone of her voice, I can still hear it, can hear her love of well-crafted sentences. We had to read Faulkner's "The Bear." It was one of his easier stories to follow, but it still was Faulkner. Those long sentences of his could have covered three chalkboards' worth of diagramming. But in Mrs. Romans' mouth, the story not only made sense; she brought out the thrill of the hunt for the old, monstrous bear named Ben. One of the hunters, Boon Hogganbeck, slits Ben's throat. I remember the sorrow that I felt when Ben died. I feel it now.

My mother, now ninety-two, lives with my family and me. She and I drink coffee together and talk about the past. She's filled in the holes of my own memories. Until recently I didn't know that after we had moved to Tennessee, Dad had decided to look for work far from home, and found it at a construction site near the state capital of Nashville, 250 miles away. He visited us every two weeks to deliver his salary to Mamá. There was a deep wanderlust in him. Except for the bimonthly visits, Dad wasn't home much during the time the relative abused me.

According to Mamá, Dad left by Greyhound bus. We waited for it at a gas station. Once he boarded it, I, six years old, said, "I hate that dog. He always takes Daddy away."

I don't remember that longing. And, as an adult, I did not say it, but Mamá: "He abandoned us." She was ninety when she said it, without bitterness, only with the sad recognition of a truth.

The construction work ended when I was around seven. Dad was, once again, unemployed. This was when we took the trip to El Salvador, and when my fixed memories of him begin—the violent moments, inexplicable, random. He was more than that, of course. But the hard times stick to us. I would come to understood the roots of his malevolence many years later. In childhood, however, they made no sense.

Once, when he was fixing the engine of our dilapidated Ford, my mother told me, "Why don't you go help your daddy?" It was, I suppose, her attempt to create a bond between father and son.

I stood next to the car. He handed me a palmful of bolts and nuts. "Hang on to them." He stuck his head back under the hood. A bolt fell out of my palm. I put the others in my pocket and crouched to the ground, but couldn't find it in the gravel. He saw me. "What are you looking for?" I told him. "You lost that fucking bolt? Son of a *bitch*!" He bent down and tossed pebbles aside. Long, excruciating minutes passed. He found it. He stared at it as though it were the most important bolt in the world, turned to me and said, "I will never trust you with anything ever again."

I had to look up to him when he said it. I was a little bigger the day of the comic books. I had a collection of almost fifty magazines, in a cardboard box full of Batman and Superman, all of them organized like files in a cabinet. It was a Sunday morning. Mamá and I had just returned from church. Dad was standing next to the outside grill. The fire reached up to the branches of a cedar tree. There was no smell of roasting meat. My box of comics was on fire. Mamá said, "Ralph, what are you doing?"

"I'm sick and tired of him." He barely looked at me. "He's always wasting time reading this shit." I could hear in his voice that he was sober.

There's a recollection that still confuses me, because it confused me at the moment. But the knife isn't memory; it's happening right now, as I write. We are in the house. I stand in the hallway. I have a small wooden train in my hand, painted blue and red. My parents are standing in the kitchen. I have to look up to see them. He's sober, and silent. I see everything from below, with my head up and my mouth open. How old am I? Seven? Eight? Because I'm small, and they're giants, though my mother shrinks before him. I don't move.

Mamá cries out to God, her voice trembling, between tears and screams. He reaches for the leather sheath that always hangs from his belt, palms the eight-inch knife and holds it up to my mother's face. He snatches her wrist. She can't escape, she can only cry and plead and shiver. Suddenly he flicks the knife at the floor. The point penetrates the yellow linoleum. The knife stands next to his shoe. He bends over, snatches the handle, jerks Mamá's arm and pulls her down the hall. When he passes, he stares down at me. Mamá screams. He drags her to their bedroom, my mother in one hand, the knife in the other. He throws her onto the bed and slams the door. It barely mutes her yelps. Or is it that he gags her with his weight, with the knife? Will he kill her? But that question does not come to mind. I don't have the vocabulary to explain what has just happened, what happens now, on the other side of the door. And so the moment ends. A moment that Mamá clarified over coffee, forty-nine years later. She told me the story. I told her I was there. "Oh my God, you remember?"

Yes, I do. And now, I have verification: There, or here, is the knife. The yellow linoleum. The woman trapped, screaming. The man without emotion.

Chapter 5

A few years ago, East Tennessee State University invited me to do a reading from one of my novels and to give a lecture on the new, growing cultural diversity in the Appalachian Mountains. They were interested in my story, one of the first Latinos to have lived in the area. They hoped I could shed light on the ethnic changes happening in the region, specifically the growing number of Latin American farmworkers who had made their homes in the eastern hills of Tennessee. I wasn't an expert, at all, on the recent community of migrant workers who seeded, cultivated, and harvested the tobacco crops. I wouldn't meet another Latino while I was there, but would stay in the confines of the university. Still, I was curious: Which community had made its home in this specific part of Appalachia? Were they Mexicans, and if so, from what region of Mexico? Or were they Salvadorans who came from my mother's hometown of Usulután? Could it be possible that I had distant family here, working in the fields and on construction sites?

My host, Landon, was a professor of Appalachian Studies at the school. He might have been a decade younger than I, perhaps in his early forties. He had a well-groomed, auburn beard. Appalachia wasn't just deep in his veins. It swirled in his brain, as though every thought he had had to do with local history, folklore, Scotch-Irish lineages that he'd traced back all the way to Derry, sharecroppers, African American Appalachians, white Appalachians, the Cherokee, and how burley tobacco, the finest ever grown, had historically played such a significant role in the region's culture. At one point, he looked embarrassed, as though having forgotten his manners. "I'm sorry, I didn't even ask if you've eaten yet."

I said I could hold off for a while, though I could sure use a cup of coffee. He chuckled and said that there were plenty of Starbucks in Johnson City, "but I reckon you're used to the gourmet kind," and kidded me about living in Los Angeles. "I'll get you a real Appalachian cup of Joe." We could, he said, go to a truck stop on the way into town. "And I've got to fill the tank."

It was a beautiful day. I hadn't seen autumn colors since moving to Los Angeles. L.A. had nothing on this blue sky, the clean wisps of clouds, and the mountains that were afire with fall colors. So beautiful; and the more I recognized that beauty, the more my nerves crackled. Perhaps, I thought, it was the public reading, and the classes I was to visit, that had suddenly put me on edge. But that wasn't it. I was, for the first time in years, in the territory where it had all happened, the ground zero of my PTSD.

Landon looked for the exit ramp to the truck stop. I stared out the window at all the beauty, then, in the rearview mirror, caught sight of a new, huge, red Dodge Ram pickup truck following behind us at a respectful distance. You couldn't help but notice it, not just because that fire-engine red stood out so much, but due to the mast that stuck out of its bed, no less than six feet tall, with a colorful sail whipping behind it, tight in the wind. What in the world was that, a pickup truck-turned-sailboat Dodge? Landon was too busy looking for the exit ramp to notice. He slowed down a bit. The truck pulled up a little closer, but still kept a safe distance from us. We were both in the right lane. Landon looked in the mirror. "What the heck is that sticking out of his bed?" I said I was wondering the same thing.

Landon pulled into the left lane to let the truck pass. The Ram, which looked the size of a Panzer, kept to its speed and slowly came up from behind us and to our side, with a crisscross of white stars and red background flickering behind the mast. The truck started to pass us. The driver, a man with a bushy blonde beard and hair, gave the informal salute of thank you to Landon and kept driving. And that Confederate flag, which was the size of a queen-sized bed sheet, whipped behind the pole. The mast was bolted into the floor. And it was indeed a sailboat's mast, strong and thick enough not to snap from the flag's violent whip. Landon glanced at it while keeping his eye on the road. He seemed embarrassed. He didn't say anything until the truck disappeared on the other side of a crest. "It's gotten worse since Charleston." He didn't need to say any more.

At the truck stop, while Landon filled the tank, I walked into the store and considered whether or not to buy a cup of muddy gas station coffee.

Along with all the snacks, candies, ice cream, sodas, beer, coffee maker, and two microwave ovens, were shelves that held knickknacks for passing tourists: key rings with a hillbilly man cut into the varnished wood, cups with the East Tennessee State University's logo printed on the side, and little maps of Tennessee that were mounted on cardboard backing.

One item stood alone on an empty shelf, something I recognized from long ago. A tiny Confederate flag dangled from a wooden rod that was barely thicker than a toothpick. It stuck out of a hole in a varnished wood base, which had, burned into its front, *Southern Pride*. When I was a kid, I passed by such shelves without giving them any thought. Back then, they were full of flags, one of those items that no one cares to buy. But this shelf, except for the one flag, was empty. I grabbed a bottle of Fiji water, which surprised me, Fiji in east Tennessee? Oh, but it was rising, all of it: the memories, the recognition of culture, the recognition of myself, the man in the pickup truck and the boy at the cash register, who suffered from a bad case of acne. I knew, so deeply, where I was, and who I was, and the reasons why I had made the decision, long ago, to leave my Appalachian world behind.

But it wasn't all about race. This was the territory I had stayed away from most of my adult life, a separation from what had happened in childhood. For some reason, this new manifestation of southern pride tapped into the old fears. Was this southern pride, or simply white rage?

The pimply cashier was on his phone, probably texting someone or posting something onto his social media. He put it down, smiled, and greeted me, asked if I was passing through or visiting kin, and rang up my water. I asked him about the empty shelf. He laughed, shook his head and said, "That thing was always full of flags until recently. Now, I can hardly keep them in stock."

For the rest of the trip, I was a bundle of nerves. Things had changed; or had they? Had it always been like this? Had such ostentatious glorification of a treasonous flag been lingering in the minds of the locals? Here I was, back in Tennessee, a place I knew so well. My childhood home was just a few miles down the 11-W highway. The field my father was born in was a twenty-minute drive away. A stone's throw. Or, as we used to say in childhood, spittin' distance.

This was the autumn of 2015. I had flown into Tennessee four months after Dylann Roof, the twenty-one-year-old white supremacist, had murdered nine African Americans during a prayer service at the Emanuel African Methodist Episcopal Church in Charleston, South Carolina. Before he had massacred the parishioners, he had posted pictures of himself on social media, rifle in hand, Nazi symbols sewn onto his jean vest, and a Confederate flag behind him.

The killings had sparked a call to action in the South. The South Carolina General Assembly voted to remove the flag from the State Capitol grounds. Other states followed suit. The US House of Representatives banned the display of Confederate flags at Veterans Administration cemeteries. Wal-Mart and Amazon announced their plans to stop selling merchandise with the flag on it. In the four months after the massacre, much of the South was making changes to distance itself from its racist history.

But someone was still manufacturing Confederate flags and selling them to a growing consumer group. I had not seen so many in all my life. Cars had bumper stickers of it. Families had their own small masts sticking at an angle out of porch posts. Kids taped little ones to their bicycle handles, like pinwheels.

Not much else had changed since my childhood. Sleepy, outsiders tended to call this region of the country—a sleepy, laid-back, quiet place, with people who sat on porch swings and called out to passersby to come up and visit for a spell. That was all still true, but those flags lay over the region like a palimpsest of silent, rebellious rage.

After the gig at ETSU, I visited my hometown of Rogersville. In retrospect, I see it was a bad idea. Why get so close to the geographic source of the abuse? But something compelled me, the insatiable need to pin it down, make sense of it, as though there were sense in violence. It all swirled in my mind: the racist flags, my enraged father, the sex abuse. They were—they *are*—all inextricably linked together. For me, the trauma in childhood doesn't stand alone. Nor does Dad's anger, nor the racial definitions taught to me when I was a kid. They are fused into one dark entity, which I have tried to pull apart, to try to understand something that is always beyond my grasp. So I drove to Rogersville for an afternoon, though I avoided the old neighborhood, and the house where it all had happened.

Rogersville hadn't changed much, hardly at all. The center of town was more desolate than I remembered, due to a Wal-Mart that stood on the edge of town. It had shut down nearly every mom and pop shop on Main Street. There weren't as many Confederate flags here, though some hung off porch railings, along with the Stars and Stripes. The Oh Henry's restaurant was open. It still served the tastiest burger I've ever put in my mouth, with just a wee bit more grease absorbed into the bun. The waitress was nice. She kept my coffee cup filled and chatted with me. "Los Angeles? Really?" she said. She had always wanted to take a trip out west and had dreamed about bumping into actors in Hollywood.

After lunch, I drove to Clinch Mountain, where my father had been born. I knew Clinch well. Dad, Mamá, and I had fished there, hunted there, and sometimes visited friends and a couple of distant kin. But that was decades ago.

Nothing had changed. No urban development, no factories or offices, or even new churches. I recognized homes from forty years back. It was Sunday afternoon. People were on their porches. Kids played football in a front yard.

The field my father was born in had no structures on it anymore. No barns, houses, or sharecropper shacks. Weeping willows grew alongside Caney Creek. A line of poplar trees stood on one edge of the field. I parked on the road's weedy shoulder, stepped—with my wingtip shoes—on rocks that stuck out from the creek, and searched for the spot. The shack was no longer there. It had been when I was a kid, dilapidated, dry-rotted. I'd never stepped foot in it, but I saw it every time Dad drove us into this section of the hollers whenever we went fishing. I had always known it was the sharecropper shack in which Dad was born. We never talked about it, at least he and I. It was Mamá who, in her Salvadoran-flavored English, pointed it out from time to time, "There's where your father came into the world." She'd shake her head, still amazed at the poverty he'd been born into, a poverty that outmatched that of her native country.

I walked into the field, straight to the place where I remembered the shack once stood. There was nothing left of it, except for the low piles of rocks that had kept the house suspended over the ground. I stood in the middle of the stones and imagined the one-room building, that I was in it, that I heard my father's first cries from 1920. I imagined my mamaw—my grandmother—cursing throughout the birth, and my grandfather standing outside, muttering Baptist prayers. Imagination took its own road: I saw a pale white baby, raised up in the arms of a midwife who slapped his fanny to get him to breathe. In my mind, his cry took on shape and meaning—somewhere in the scream came forth squeaky, newborn words, *Goddamn motherfucking son of a bitch*. Words that were all too familiar, words that I had heard all through childhood, regarding whatever it was that needed to be cursed: a fish hook caught on a rock, a broken carburetor, the government, a lost bolt. Where did such an image come from, that of a newborn cursing the world the moment he took his first breath?

Born in that shack in the middle of a desolate field, Dad, as did all children of sharecroppers, worked the tobacco alongside his father. Sharecroppers got paid only once a year, at harvest time. The system had been created shortly after the Civil War, a replacement for the free labor of African American slaves. Yes, the rich farmer now had to pay both his white and black employees, all who lived in their own shacks, but it was a pittance.

My papaw—my grandfather—worked the crop from March to November. He had to buy his own tools on credit, along with food and farm supplies. After selling the tobacco, he took the wad of money down to Main Street in Rogersville and paid off all his creditors. Then he handed over more than half the rest to the landowner. He slipped the remaining slim bills into his wallet and talked about game, that the deer, hopefully, would be thick and get them through the winter. But they had known starvation. Dad started using tobacco as a toddler, out of necessity. Mamaw stuck tobacco leaves into her son's mouth in order to calm the hunger pangs.

The woods nearby the field where Dad was born are only a couple of miles from the house that I grew up in. The moments I did feel close to Dad were when he took me hunting, fishing, and camping. As long as he stayed sober, we had a pretty good time. He taught me how to bait a hook and load a shotgun, how to scale a bass and skin a rabbit. Out there, on a creek bank or in a tree stand, he spoke more to me, whispering while we waited for game to come our way. In the woods, he felt free. But when we returned home, he avoided me.

*

As I stood in the field where Dad was born, I considered all the Confederate flags. A chill shot through me. I saw, as though through a dark mirror, a connection between my father's anger and the cross of stars. But he wasn't the flag-waving type. And he could never have afforded such a luxurious truck as the one with the sailboat mast.

Still, there was a connection. All those flags, waving under the shadow of a race-based massacre in Charleston. Such audacity—no, such rebellion—no, not that either. There are places where my imagination cannot go. I witness white hate, one that rises from a people who have felt crushed ever since losing the Civil War. I get it. Then I don't. All the hatred that raises those flags looks too similar to my father's rage. Maybe that's why I can't understand: I'm too close to the subject. Maybe that's why I no longer lie about my father, painting him before others as a good-old-boy. He wasn't good, nor bad; he was broken. I've wondered how his own past, his own suffering in childhood, infected my own.

There is a whisper of this theory that comes out of memory—not mine, but my father's. In the 1930s, when he was fifteen, he had hoboed across the country, joining two hundred thousand men, women, and children who sought jobs and adventure during the Great Depression. He jumped into cargo boxes, avoided the train police, and spent nights in hobo camps alongside the tracks.

Once, when he was in his sixties, Mamá, Dad, and I took a road trip into Kentucky. We stopped at a small town because Dad wanted to see a bridge, one he had slept under, along with two dozen other hoboes, fifty years before. "Yeah, this is it," he said. He didn't walk into its shadow. He stood to one side and only said, "Bad things went on under there." Then it happened—his head rattled, jerked to one side with the memory, a head jerk that happens to me whenever the relative rushes my mind.

The relative's sexual moves on me were so very adult. It was as though he had been taught. There was only one person in the house who could have shown him that. I wondered if the violence, the "bad things" under the bridge, had happened to Dad when he was a teenager, in a hobo camp where older men held on to their "queens," the teenage boys and girls who kept them satisfied. I wondered if the sins of 1935, against him, shot through the decades and landed on the relative. Had Dad abused him? Was my kin imitating the movements of my father, against me? But when he had confessed to me over the phone, I asked him, point blank, "Did my dad do it to you?" He said that no, my father had never touched him. This throws my theory, for he said it sincerely, as though having pondered it a long while.

There are some questions that can't be answered. There is no explanation to *Why did it happen?* I put the pieces together as best I can and sometimes get a glimpse of understanding. Then, like that, it's gone.

That trip, however, opened up something in me—a certain empathy toward my father. Even with all that Confederate hate flapping in the wind, I could see a little more of who he was. He had been dead a number of years before the gig at ETSU. I had been by his side in his last days. He was ninety-one when he passed. He had quit drinking twenty years before. We had made a certain peace with each other, though the distance between us was still there.

It was the standing in the field that made me see that, what had happened in my childhood had tainted all of the mountains. I think on it now—there's a certain tragedy to all this. An entire, beautiful region, hurled into the thick, cold shadows of one relative's actions.

I couldn't stay any longer in the field. I flew back home to LA. That was several years ago. I haven't been back to those Appalachian Mountains since then. That was a loss. But now, looking back, it seemed inevitable.

Chapter 6

Mamá's slippers sweep across the white oak floor. Her walker clomps slightly as she passes over a thin rise between her bedroom and the hallway. It's ten o'clock; she's just woken up. Actually, she woke up an hour ago, but it takes that much time for her to get out of bed and dress. She makes her way to the kitchen, where she will, on her own, smear peanut butter over a piece of toast, boil the water for her instant coffee, place the plate and cup on the walker's seat and carry them to the table. While she's doing that, I clean her porta-potty in her bedroom.

At ninety-two, she's still able to do small things, like making her own breakfast, or putting laundry into the washer, though Michelle or I have to transfer them to the dryer, as the wet clothes are too heavy for her to manage.

She eats fairly well. I make her a sandwich at midday. Sometimes she eats only half, but other times I praise her for cleaning the plate. I take her dishes away. In the beginning she told me she could do it herself, but she's gotten weaker, so I pick up some of the slack. She spends most of the day watching television. She's gotten quieter since moving in with us three years ago. We don't talk as much about the past. It's as though we've exhausted it after so many coffee conversations.

I take her outside on pretty days. It's a pure dance. There's a small step from the back door to the ground, but for her, it's a precipice. We hold each other's arms. I walk backwards as she negotiates the steps. Once we're on the ground, we have another goal: get to her chair, which is right behind me. We tango toward it. Once she's in front of it, I snake my arms under her armpits. She grabs the chair's armrests. Together, we set her down. Sometimes she plops, and usually laughs about it then lightly curses old age.

I sit with her. Minutes of silence—a fairly comfortable silence—will pass before we start talking about the new flowers Michelle had planted on the edge of the property. "It takes time," she says when I worry about whether or not they're dying. "Just be patient. Before you know it, you'll have to prune them back."

She's not the same woman who raised me. In all of the culture-love that she gave me in childhood, with all the Salvadoran food and dancing, she also had a rage in her that, in her own words, came out of nowhere. It had been with her since her years in high school back in El Salvador. It was the same unleashed fury her grandmother and mother had, an ire that meant to set the world straight by scaring it half to death. But she has none of that rage now. Still, I feel it. I feel that angry mother of childhood, something to contend with. Sometimes her very presence turns against me.

Manic depression is genetic and can be passed down from one generation to the next. Some of our Villatoro ancestors were known back in the Old Country as *los locos*. They lived on a farm on the edge of Usulután, where supposedly they rode horses bareback with hardly any clothes on. They yelled for no reason, and fell into heaps of melancholy, usually with a bottle of cheap liquor in their hands. We had our poets and revolutionaries, hospitalizations and suicides. And, not ironically, some of those crazy ancestors grew up to be one ambassador, two professors, and a boss at the Singer sewing machine company (many bipolars tend to be, when not ill, very high achievers).

Once, in a sudden twist of memory, Mamá confessed to putting a gun to her head. It blurted out of her, like a frantic confession. It was in Tennessee, years before she had me. Dad was outside, flirting with an old girlfriend. Life had become too much—the inner world of the illness joined with the stress of living in a foreign land where she could hardly speak. She had a husband who would spend the rest of their married life jumping from one woman's bed to another's. She regretted: she should have stayed in El Salvador, should have never looked into his green eyes. She put the muzzle to the side of her head and cocked back the hammer. The *click* rattled her. She chose to live.

Dad died a decade ago. It's given Mamá time to reconsider their lives together. She loved him, but she doesn't say that much anymore, as though she has no more use for protecting him. She talks about his womanizing.

She once said, "He was . . . rough, in bed." She speaks about his drunkenness. It's not quite bitterness. I wonder if it's a type of mourning, not over his death, but over her own life.

*

I struggle with her still. Though she doesn't blow up anymore, sometimes the resonance of her acrid, mean-spirited voice from my childhood cracks through. I remember once having to make a play-banjo for a grade school skit. I painted the lines of strings with a thick brush. It turned out a mess of long black splotches down the neck. She looked at it. I saw it coming on, in that split-second: the rage. "That looks like shit! SHIT!" She turned and walked away. Then she returned, and I could see it—the remorse, though she didn't apologize, as though she didn't know how to. I don't judge her for it, now that I know we share the illness.

We all know those certain movements in our family member's faces, the slight tweak of a cheek muscle, the raised eyebrow, the mouth pulled up to one side in disdain. One slight crinkle in my mother's brow can set me off, the same crinkle that once preceded an explosion of rage. But she doesn't rage, not anymore. I made sure of that when she moved in. She takes a medicine similar to one of mine. It's made all the difference. It's the reason why she doesn't attack. And she's happy now, grateful for our caregiving. She's surrounded by people who love her.

The decision to take her in happened in a snap, because she did something right. After my father died and she still lived in Tennessee, I had visited her from time to time, which was never easy, having to step into that house, where I slept on the couch rather than dare to enter the back bedroom, where it had happened. We were talking about the past, specifically about the relative, and what he had done to me. Decades before, I had confronted both her and Dad about what had happened, in a barbaric yawp of rage. Now, sitting in her kitchen, we spoke of it quietly. She regretted that she had not done anything about it. I said, to assuage her guilt (Why? I have no idea, except for the training I had gotten in childhood—to appease the ones who betray you in order to stave off an attack), "Well, he was very, sneaky. He made sure you all were asleep."

She dropped her head slightly toward the table. "No," she said, "it was my fault. I wasn't watching close enough. And your father and I, we drank, too much . . ." Her voice trailed off. But she had said it. She recognized her own culpability and spilled it out. Then she did the second thing right: she didn't ask me for forgiveness. There were no strings attached to her atonement. This freed me; for forgiveness can be a violent thing for a survivor. To be asked to do it is a trap, and a way of getting the guilty off the hook. To some, this may sound like bitterness. It is, in part. But it's more than that. Forgiveness can turn against the victim. It's as though someone were saying, *You've just got to let it go*. That, to me, is another form of brutality.

Mamá didn't ask for forgiveness. She simply apologized.

I said I had to lie down for a bit, that I was tired from the plane ride. She took our cups to the sink. I lay on the couch but didn't sleep. It all swirled in my mind, what she had just said. Something snapped open—clarity. I called Michelle. We talked about it. We had talked about it before, since my father's death. We worried about her living alone. But both of us knew what effect my mother could have on me if we lived together. Over the phone I told Michelle what had happened. She understood, but said, "Are you sure about this?"

Was I sure? Not completely. But I loved the woman. She had done her best as a mother. And now, she had laid her burdens down before me, with no strings attached.

"I think I can do this."

Michelle was happy. She had always wanted to take care of our parents in their old age. But she was wary. "We've got to make sure you don't get sick." I told her I would be careful. And, starting now, I'd put my foot down. It seemed to assuage her worries. She said yes.

We hung up. I turned to Mamá. "Let's sit down a minute." We did. I leaned toward her, my hands clasped together, my voice as authoritative as it had ever been with her. "If I let you move in with us, will you behave?"

She knew what I meant. She promised up and down, "Oh yes, yes, I'll be good!" The invitation was too much; she smiled so hard I thought it would crack her face in two.

I knew that telling her to behave wouldn't be enough. You can't change genetics with a simple warning. Five days after she moved in with us—five days of her hot temper that again came out of nowhere—we visited my doctor. He diagnosed her, possible bipolar II, with the sudden fluctuations of moods that had haunted her all her life. He prescribed the medication. It took a few weeks to kick in. When it did, I said to Michelle, "If only she'd taken it years ago." Michelle agreed; or she thought she agreed. Because she said, "She wouldn't have suffered so much." I wasn't thinking about that. I was considering how that pill could have made a big difference in my life, my childhood. I'm a survivor. I must think this way.

*

Mamá is a survivor. She was born into a rich family named Reyes who owned a coffee plantation that covered three mountains. A man shot her father, Pilar, when she was two. Supposedly it had to do with a lowdown rapscallion who had taken my grandfather's sister to bed out of wedlock, though Mamá suspects that there was more to the story.

The night after Pilar was murdered, her mother, Romilia, took her away from the Reyes family and delivered her to my great grandmother Martina, who shouted out what everyone in the neighborhood believed, "Those bastards killed this girl's father and they're going to kill her next!"

She may have had a point. The Reyes family hated Romilia. They saw her as lowdown trash that had shacked up with their son. My mother was a threat—she might, as she got older, demand her part of the inheritance. But there was no inheritance, because Abuelita, eighteen at the time, signed a letter that the Reyes family had written up, promising that she would never demand to receive any money or land.

Not that she needed it. Though they weren't wealthy, the Villatoros did well enough on their own. They were in much better shape than my father's family in Tennessee. They owned a small store. Everyone cowered before my great grandmother. Old Martina was loud and sick with the family illness, but she dealt with it in her own way by staying busy from four in the morning to ten at night, baking sweet breads, making cheese, selling fresh tortillas and pupusas. Still, she was, my mother said, always yelling, and cursed as though having spent years with sailors.

Mamá's grandfather, Papa Polo, was not ill in the least. While Martina raged and made more money than anyone in the barrio, Papa Polo took care of the kids—not just my mother, but a half dozen other children of maids who worked for them. As furious as she was, Martina opened her home to single, pregnant women. It was a fair exchange: She gave them a room to give birth in, then gave them jobs. The women stacked Martina's wares on wide, shallow baskets and balanced them on their heads while walking through town, calling out, "Pan dulce, queso fresco, cigarillos!" So many kids running around the house; my mother remembers that fondly, having all the playmates a child could want. And she had Papa Polo, who was quiet yet firm, who spent his mornings reading the Bible in the rose garden but who never preached about it. He sat with the children as they ate, and taught them good manners.

And he had books.

Today, in my library, Mamá's childhood encyclopedia collection *El tesoro de la juventud* (The Treasure of Youth) is displayed prominently on one high shelf. It's over one hundred years old. I thumb through some of the volumes from time to time, imagining my mother doing the same when she was five, when she first learned to read, when she first fell in love with books.

Chapter 7

Mamá struggled against her own illness to be as good a mother as possible. I remember her throwing a large birthday party for me when I was little. Twenty kids crowded around a piñata that she had made out of paper mâché. She was patient as she helped the children cover their eyes with a kerchief, handed the stick over and stepped quickly out of the way. The piñata fascinated the Appalachian kids. They'd never seen one in their lives.

The party was *alegre*, joyful, Salvadoran, with songs from the Old Country playing on a record player in the background. She led us all in the Happy Birthday song. I remember her doing a solo, when she sang the Spanish version of the song, *Estas son las mañanitas que cantaba el rey David*. . . . The strange words captivated my friends (this was before the elementary school years, when they weren't so steeped in racial thinking).

She was, in retrospect, a woman who struggled mightily to be a good mom, who fought against her own moods in order to raise me. She loved me. If it weren't for the family illness, my memories wouldn't feel so confused. A loving, coddling mother in one moment, enraged woman in the next. Still, I see now that she tried. She wanted the best for me.

When I turned fourteen, she sent me away. It wasn't just her idea; my grandmother in San Francisco was in agreement, that I, a bright boy, should get out of the confines of Rogersville and go to a private high school. Dad was gone again, this time working in the coal mines of Kentucky. It was the best job he had ever gotten, with a salary of sixteen thousand a year. The money could stretch, enough to cover tuition.

My mother wanted me out of Rogersville. There was, she said, no future there for me. It seemed strange at first. She had, after so many years of living in east Tennessee, made her home there. The racism of the past hadn't necessarily cleared up, but it wasn't the same. She had made many friends. She had gotten a job at the local vocational school as a secretary, and ended up pretty much running the place. She taught Spanish classes on the side in the basement of the Catholic church, which brought in a little more income. Several people showed up for them. Now, people didn't treat her as a strange outsider, but as a member of the community.

But she wanted more for me. She expected me to thrive, which meant going Out There, into a world that was much larger than my hometown. College—I could be the first in both families to attend. Not that young people from Rogersville didn't go to college; many of them matriculated at the University of Tennessee in Knoxville. But there was a strong streak of ambition in the Villatoro mind, and she passed that on to me. She said I could do better than UT; she imagined me attending an Ivy League college.

I wasn't ready to leave. I was a new teenager. Life had gotten better at home. Dad was far away, in a coal shaft. Years before, the relative had moved out. The house became a quiet place. I was a latchkey kid, which I liked. While Mamá worked, I let myself into the house, put Elton John's "Goodbye Yellow Brick Road" on the record player, made myself a snack, and did my homework, all before five o'clock, when reruns of Gilligan's Island came on. With my father and the relative gone, I felt calm.

When my mother proposed the idea of sending me off, I balked. Then we visited the Catholic high school in Knoxville, over an hour away. We spoke with the nuns and lay teachers, and spent a lunch with the principal, a huge, rotund priest named Weber who was impressed that my mother wanted more for me, so much that she was willing to let me go. The school had a large library. The students wore uniforms. It was a whole different world, one that would prove to be more scholarly than the high school of my home town.

Mamá couldn't drive me to the school, making an hour and a half trip twice a day. It wasn't a boarding school, but Father Weber had an idea: I could live with families whose kids attended Knoxville Catholic High. He found me a home, with a family who was known to be pillars of the Catholic community. My parents paid them rent. I would live my freshman year with the Hoffmans. Their youngest son, Barry, was a senior. I could stay with them until he graduated, when the Hoffmans would have no more connection with the school. It was in that house where I learned how to pray with an intensity that could have put Jesus in Gethsemane to shame.

Mr. Hoffman was a defense lawyer and made enough money so Mrs. Hoffman could stay home. They had put three children through the school. Barry was their fourth. They were hard-core church goers; even the flu couldn't keep them out of the pews. They were plugged into the Knoxville Catholic High community. Mrs. Hoffman volunteered for school fundraisers. Mr. Hoffman was the chairman of the PTA.

They were a tall family. Mrs. and Mrs. Hoffman were nearly six feet tall. Barry beat them by a couple of inches. He was lithe, with long, thick, blonde hair that he parted down the middle in the style of the late 1970s. Mr. Hoffman was a bit overweight. He had the habit of pulling at his belt, and talked a lot about losing a few pounds. Mrs. Hoffman smoked a couple of cigarettes a day and somehow kept it from smelling up her sparkling-clean home. They were nice, though a little stiff. They didn't have much of the southern porch-welcoming in them, but this made sense: I was in Knoxville, which was, to me, a metropolis. People were, I figured, more sophisticated here.

Mrs. Hoffman showed me my bedroom on the second floor, just across the hall from Barry's. It was far nicer than mine in Rogersville, with cream-colored curtains and a dark oak floor. The window faced a small park across the street.

She made us a different breakfast every day: eggs and bacon one morning, pancakes the next, oatmeal on Wednesdays. She was kind, and the one in control of the house. A little bit of the *mandona* was in her, my mother might say—the one who gives the orders. Mr. Hoffman, a quiet man, didn't seem to mind.

Barry wasn't so nice. He didn't shake my hand when I first moved in, and he rarely spoke to me. Perhaps, I thought, it was a natural disdain between senior and freshman. Or maybe I had taken his place as the youngest child. It made no sense; he seemed to have hated me from the day I'd first walked through their door. He ignored me at meals, even when I tried to make small talk with him.

After a couple of weeks of this, I became his target. Barry kept me in terror all that year. It started with my bedroom. When I wasn't around, he vandalized it. He rifled through the dresser drawers and threw all my clothes onto the floor. He knocked books and papers off the desk, pulled the sheets off the bed, unplugged all the lamps and my radio. I didn't understand; what had I done? I had moved in. That's what it must be, I thought. Though I didn't give it much thought. I was too busy defending myself from his attacks.

One night, while I was sitting at my desk, he stormed in, pulled down his shorts, showed me his buttocks, and ordered me to kiss them. I didn't move. His anger rose. He turned his senior class ring over, putting the jewel above his palm, and popped the top of my head with it, like a tiny sap. He grumbled a whisper, "Watch it boy. I'll have you kissing my dick some night."

I slept little in that house. Whenever I took the Greyhound bus home once a month back to Rogersville, my mother wondered if I was smoking marijuana, considering how many naps I took throughout the weekend. I never told her about Barry.

For weeks he popped my skull with his ring, and constantly called me a queer. I wasn't sure what a queer was, until Barry explained, "You little faggot queer, wanting to kiss other boys and get at their dicks." Always followed by his senior class ring against my skull.

Sometime before the winter holidays, I woke up in the middle of the night to a sound. I didn't move, but opened my eyes. I was completely awake, as though some strange, cold liquid had poured through me, lifting every muscle from sleep.

Barry stood next to the bed, hovering over me, a shadow. He wore only underwear. He didn't budge, as though considering a decision. His breath was shallow. Then he turned and walked out.

The following morning, we drove to school. He said nothing. I stared out the passenger side window, at the stores and fast-food restaurants. I knew not to move, not to clear my throat, and certainly not to speak.

He fisted his hand and slammed the top of my skull. Other blows followed, interrupted only by his need to change the car's gears. He didn't just use his fist; his whole arm swung down like a baseball bat. I shielded the top of my head with my arms. He kept punching. The fury didn't end until the even pulse of fourth gear. Nor did the words, "You fucking faggot! Faggot! Goddamned FAGGOT!"

*

I started to take on spiritual OCD qualities, all in the name of protecting myself. I had learned in religion class that the number seven is holy, for whatever reason. The number became part of my own personal liturgy. My tics were tiny movements: I clicked my teeth together seven times, and lightly tapped my forehead with my left index finger knuckle seven times, which I'm sure looked a little strange, a teenager lowering his head slightly and hitting his forehead as though knocking on a door. These were rituals that I hoped would keep Barry at bay, as though the tapping on the forehead was a small sacrifice that would take the place of his head bashing.

That January, one of the Hoffmans' daughters got married. In order to provide for the out-of-town families, Mrs. Hoffman had me stay in Barry's room, in a second bed that was once one of his siblings'. After the wedding and reception, the family gathered downstairs and kept the party going. I stayed in the crowd all night, until Barry went to bed. An hour later, I made my way upstairs, hoping he was asleep. I opened the door slowly to keep the hinges from creaking. The lights were off. He was in his bed, his back to me. I tiptoed to the second bed. He said, in a low voice, "If you make one noise I swear I will kill you."

I nodded, as though he could see me, and reached for the blanket. There was something on the bed, a large object. It was Barry's guitar. I slowly, carefully, took it by the lower end of the neck and lifted it. A metal object slid down the strings, hit my hand and fell to the wood floor.

Barry jumped out of his bed, threw me to the floor and sat on my pelvis. He locked me between his thighs. He knew where to punch: only in the abdomen, one side and the other. He beat me until his lungs gave out, climbed off me and got back in his bed. I lay there for I don't know how long, waiting, listening to his breaths, holding my stomach as though to keep the guts from falling out.

I still had to deal with the guitar. I picked it up, looked for a place to put it, then leaned it into a corner. I stepped on something, reached down and picked it up. It was the long, sixteen-penny nail that he had placed on the guitar strings.

I crawled into bed. Downstairs, the party went on.

*

I actually believed that my head-knuckling had worked—he hadn't bashed my skull that night, but had punched my stomach. Perhaps, I figured, my OCD prayers hadn't made it clear enough for God to get it. What was needed was more explicit prayer.

Father Weber celebrated mass every morning. Mostly the nuns showed up, though there was a scattering of students as well. I joined them. That first morning, when Barry parked in the school's lot, I ran to the building. "Where the hell you going?" he asked. I turned quickly and told him that I wanted to make it to mass. He said nothing.

I attended every morning service. But that wasn't enough. In the afternoons, during study hall, I asked the teacher if I could be excused. When she first asked why, I mumbled that I wanted to go pray. The teacher smiled and allowed me to leave.

I went to the chapel. At two-thirty I prayed for the hour of three-fifteen, when Barry would take us home. I didn't pray to God for Divine Intervention, though that would have been nice. I had made an A in religion class, where Sister Evelyn taught us to be above such petitions. We were, she said, responsible for most of the events around us. We couldn't blame God for the bad moments in our lives.

I took this to heart and prayed to God that He help me do all the right things so that Barry's wrath would end. May God help me say the correct words to appease Barry, or to know when to say no words at all. May God help me have the silent strength to withstand the knuckles and ring. Dear God, grant me the profound silence of tranquility and lack of movement if Barry were to stand over my bed again.

One afternoon, as I left study hall, another student named Carmen asked for permission to go to the bathroom. I would have thought little of this, until I heard the chapel door open. She walked in. I was sitting on the left, three pews from the altar. "Am I bothering you?" she asked.

I looked up at her. Carmen was my age, fourteen. She had long black hair and slightly sleepy eyes. She was thin, and played on the girls' basketball team. "No," I said, and invited her to sit down. Though worried about how I would get through my prayer rituals before the bell rang—including the teeth clicking and forehead tapping—I also welcomed the company.

"I noticed that you always leave study hall. And Mrs. Gibbons lets you go. I guess I just got curious."

I smiled, embarrassed yet appreciative of her curiosity, that she actually found me worthy of it. "So," she said, "you come here to pray."

"Oh, yeah, kind of, I guess," I responded in the eloquence befitting a freshman. "Sometimes I just like to sit. It's nice and quiet in here."

"Yeah, some say you're pretty religious." There was no tone of mockery to it. The words sounded respectful. It also surprised me that I was the subject of such gossip. "I heard a few teachers saying that you'll probably become a priest."

I chuckled, but then gave it some serious thought. The idea had occurred to me before. Hearing Carmen say it made it more real.

"So," she asked, "what do you pray for?"

It stopped me cold. I couldn't answer, but wanted to. I wanted to tell her everything. How I prayed for strength to withstand the upcoming evening. How I prayed that Mr. and Mrs. Hoffman would not go out to a church council meeting or dinner with friends, leaving me in the house with Barry. How I clicked my teeth and tapped my forehead to the Almighty so that Barry would not visit me at night. I wanted to say all this to get a secret message across to her, one that she could take to some authorities such as her parents, who would then report it and save me from another night.

But I said none of it. I didn't, knowing that to stir the waters meant to put the venerated Hoffman family into question. Yet they would not be questioned, for they were the Hoffmans, beloved by the Catholic community. I was just a kid from a tiny hillbilly town in the Appalachian Mountains. To speak meant to be sent back to Rogersville in shame and failure.

Though I remained silent, my look gave me away. The glisten of tears welled in my eyes.

"Are you okay?" Carmen asked.

"Oh, I'm fine," I said, but the tears were coming on. "I guess . . . I just miss my parents."

"Yeah, I bet that's really hard." She went on about how difficult it must be to live so far away from home, but I was lucky to be with the Hoffmans. "They're such a nice family."

She touched my shoulder with a limp hand, smiled at me, said goodbye and walked out.

The bell rang. I jumped from the pew, genuflected, shot out of the chapel, collected my books in study hall, then ran to my locker. I cut through a block of students and bolted outside toward the parking lot, where Barry walked casually with a few of his senior friends. While crossing the school yard toward the cars, I rattled off the words that I would have said seven times in the quietude of the chapel had not Carmen interrupted me. I balanced my books in one hand so as to tap my forehead with the other, all the while clicking my teeth. I remember my prayer, one that I had honed into a near-canonical petition: "Dear Lord, may your love burn in my heart so that I may be a sign of your life on earth. Please may I have your Holy Strength to endure the ride home, then the afternoon and evening, until I speak with you again before sleep. If I fail in endurance, may Your mercy be upon me."

*

Even though I didn't pray for Barry to drop dead, the next best thing happened: In the spring he got mononucleosis. It knocked him out of school. He stayed most days in bed, dragging himself downstairs only to try to eat. He lay on the couch and watched television with his mother. Mr. Hoffman took me to school. It was a wondrous time. All I had to deal with were Barry's comments that he slung at me, weakly, from his bedroom. Goddamn faggot. Queer. Asshole. "Whose dick did you suck today?" After a while, the mono set in deep. His voice turned weaker. Sleep took him over.

The day after the school year ended, my mother picked me up to take me home for the summer. This was a final goodbye to the Hoffmans. I would never see them again. Mrs. Hoffman reached down and hugged me, said I was such a good boy, and cried a little. Mr. Hoffman shook my hand and wished me the best. Barry was upstairs. He had gotten a little better by this time. He didn't want to come down. Mrs. Hoffman went up. I had to retrieve my suitcase. Halfway up the stairs I heard her, "Go downstairs and shake that boy's hand."

"I don't want to." Said in a snarky, leave-me-alone-Mom voice.

But she didn't leave him alone. I stood there on a middle step and heard it so clearly, I still hear it now. "The way you've treated him all year long, you at least could have the decency to say goodbye."

Chapter 8

The summer after my freshman year, in recollection, seems uneventful, and quiet. Dad was still working in the coal mines. It was just my mother and me in the house. I don't remember her losing control of her emotions as she had done in earlier years, no sudden bursts of rage followed by remorse. She worked all day long. I had a lot of time to myself, something I've cherished ever since—a few hours of solitude, every day, when I don't need to gauge the moods and actions of others.

She and I enjoyed each other's company. We cooked together, watched television together, and went fishing a couple of times. I spent time with my childhood friend Blake, who had a car and a driving permit. He wasn't supposed to drive around without an adult in the car, but the two local policemen were lax about it. We cruised with all the other teenagers in town. It was a normal summer, as far as I can remember. Then, in August, I moved back to Knoxville to begin my sophomore year.

I moved in with the Tanners. They were some of the quietest people I had ever met. No one raised their voice in that house. They were kind, proper, and sophisticated. No curse words, no surreptitious violence. Mr. Tanner had the beard of a Viking. Mrs. Tanner, a stout, portly woman, cooked every night. We ate precisely at 6 p.m. They too had their last child, Anne, in Knoxville Catholic. She was a senior, which meant I would stay with them for a year. She had a few light freckles on her cheeks, which I found attractive. She usually wore her long, dirty-blonde hair in a ponytail.

I fell in love with Anne, with her goodness. It had been her idea to take me in. I suppose that, after enough badgering (she was good at that), she talked her parents into it. I don't doubt she regretted it later, having a hang-dog sophomore mooning over her day and night. But she had been good to me, a balm, even though I hadn't told her much about what had happened with Barry, except to say that he was a bit of a bully.

I was exhausted much of the time. Only now do I see the reasons. Freshman year with the Hoffmans, with Barry, had been a continuation of childhood, of the duck-and-cover, obsequious, good-boy character that I had formed into a shield. With the Tanners, I could let go of those defense mechanisms, though I didn't, not completely. Survivors of childhood abuse will spend a lifetime looking over their shoulder. The muscles of the mind remain taut with fight-or-flight, and they stay in that strained position long after the threat is over.

But in the Tanner house, I felt relatively secure. There were no surprises. They followed a scheduled life, which helped a great deal. I could count on a hearty breakfast before school, a day of studies without any threats, afternoon homework, the 6 p.m.-sharp supper, an hour of television with the family, then having the rest of the evening to myself. They were well-to-do and owned a large house in west Knoxville, the upper-class side of town. I not only had my own bedroom downstairs, but a private bathroom as well.

They were good. Their ground was solid, and safe to walk on. No threats, no raised voices, no sadistic, homophobic teenager. I could breathe easily. I could rest. My mind turned lax. A weariness took over, as though my fifteen-year-old mind were telling me, *Here, with these people, you're safe.*

But the exhaustion had no floor to it. I dropped into a bottomless pit. I trace my early depressive tendencies back to sophomore year. Of course that was the year: In all that goodness, in the safe confines of a healthy family, even though I couldn't articulate it, my mind roiled in the past. It tried to make sense of it all and, finding none, turned inward. A lifelong battle with depression was just beginning.

Though I don't remember the initial pain, I can still see the half-inch of blood in the peach-colored sink. I held the knife in my left hand. It was a large pocketknife. When I was a kid, Dad had shown me how to keep a blade honed. I knew how to spit on a whetstone and pull the blade over the lowering belly of the stone back and forth, collecting a fine mix of spittle and grain with the blade's edge before stropping it with a leather belt. I had not cut downward, from my hand toward my elbow, but across. The blood didn't spurt; it dribbled thick from the wound.

I dropped the knife, placed my left palm over the wound and held it there, applying pressure, just as we sophomores had all been taught in the recent high school first aid training. It took a quarter of a roll of toilet paper to daub the cut. Blood stains were on the cabinet. Some had splashed onto the ceramic tile floor.

Please forgive me, Lord. I don't want to die.

I needed to clean the blood from everything, flush it all down the toilet, then take a cleaning rag and pine cleaner disinfectant to the entire bathroom. It took time. I worked like a panicking murderer.

With one last swipe over the counter, I looked into the mirror. My black hair sat on my skull like a used mop. My skin had turned pasty. I covered the cut with two bandages, pulled my long sleeve over it, left the bathroom and fell upon my bed. I turned my radio on then glanced over at the large picture window that faced the driveway. Anne's Volkswagen wasn't there. No doubt she had left the house within the past hour, since our encounter upstairs, the encounter that I would, for a while, blame for my actions.

I stared at a poster on the wall in front of me. John Travolta, twenty-four years old and dressed in a white, open-collar suit and black boots, stood in his pelvis-strutting, finger-piercing-the-sky position, staring down at me with the look of disco perfection. A strobe ball dangled above him. "Saturday Night Fever," a movie I had seen three times. It was, to me, the most magnificent film ever created by humankind. I wanted the poster to absorb me.

The disco jockey on the pop radio station played, probably for the seventh time that day, the Bee Gees' "How Deep Is Your Love?" I listened to the words. For the first time in a month, the song didn't make me weep. I didn't feel the thickening sadness fill me, along with the Brothers Gibb's mellifluous, slow-disco song.

I remembered a lesson from history class, how they believed in George Washington's time that bleeding oneself was a way to get rid of certain diseases. Had I bled the melancholy out of my body? I closed my eyes, listening to the three singers as they tried, with all their romantic might, to penetrate my skull with a wash of tears.

*

I had fallen in love with Anne because of her goodness. I had not realized how much the previous year with the Hoffman family had affected me. In the Tanner house, I felt the barricade of well-constructed defenses shatter around my feet. Their home had become a sanctuary.

In my first month with them, I had partly told Anne about the year with Barry. I didn't mention his sexual threats, fearing that, somehow, it would shadow her thoughts about me rather than him, as though I were in part to blame for his actions.

She listened. She even wept. Then she hugged me and whispered, "This is your home. You're safe now." The hug, and her listening, and her kindness, along with the sweet perfume that she splashed against her neck, was my undoing. My heart plopped out of my chest. Through that winter it wriggled perpetually before her feet. I followed her in the school hallways. I stared at her at suppertime. After a while I started looking for other problems in my life so that she would have to listen to me. When that didn't work, I made problems up: living away from home, not doing well in a class, a friend with whom I'd had an argument. Anything to keep her attention.

She began to shut me out. She spent less time at home, dashing off in her car to a music or dance lesson, or to a party with her senior friends. She avoided me at breakfast, dropping her head toward her bowl of oatmeal.

The day that I drew the pocketknife over my wrist was the day that I had come to her with the truth. "I love you," then added, shakily, "I'm in love with you." She, of course, did not love me, not in that way. She had been kind about it, but made it clear. I could hear the impatience in her voice. Then she had left, and I ran down the stairs to my room and took the knife out of the dresser drawer.

I hid the wound, wearing long sleeves all the time, even during the warm spring days. I don't know if the Tanners suspected. All I knew at the time was, I would never, ever do it again.

*

In June, Anne graduated. My sophomore year ended. It was time to leave the fast streets of Knoxville and return to the slow roads of my hometown. I had to say goodbye to Anne. She was good about it, gave me a firm hug, then patted my shoulder. After that, she was gone, spending time at parties with her fellow graduates.

That first morning of summer break, I didn't get out of bed. My mother walked in. I had the covers over my head. She sat on the edge of the bed, figured out where my arm was underneath the cover and gently placed her hand over my wrist. Though it was down against the mattress, it jumped, as if the healed cut had suddenly wriggled.

So, she had known. I had hidden the scar as best I could, but I couldn't keep wearing long-sleeved shirts all summer long. I kept my arms to my sides to keep the cut hidden. It didn't work. When had she first seen it? She hadn't questioned me about it, hadn't yelled at me out of fear or anger or both. That's all I thought about: I would get in trouble for what I had done. I had worried about this all through the spring, believing that, had anyone seen it, they would have reported me to Principal Weber. But no one had said anything.

Mamá spoke about getting me some help. I shivered at that. My worst nightmare was about to come: She would send me off to a psychologist for testing, or worse, commit me to an asylum. I had expected her to fire questions at me: Why was I so sad all the time? Why didn't I want to get out of bed? Would I look for a summer job? She asked none of that. Instead, she said, "I've got an idea, *mi hijo*." My son. Whenever she used a Spanish word with me, it was to show love. "Let's go to San Francisco for the summer." She said she was quitting her job at the vocational school. (Did she do that for my sake?) She talked about the prospects of spending three months on the West Coast, that we could be with family for a while, stay with my grandmother, and see the sites. San Francisco. My birth-city . . . why there? It was as though she knew, long before I did, that my hometown could somehow save me.

Chapter 9

As there was a trajectory of abuse in my first fifteen years—the relative, my father, Barry's brutality—so was there a path of strength: My childhood in San Francisco; the trip at age seven to El Salvador; the summer back in my home city. I didn't recognize it at the time, didn't see how my Latino self was saving me from a turbulent childhood. All I saw was disco.

My Villatoro cousins, most of them in their early twenties, took me out dancing two, sometimes three times a week. Aunt Marina bought me a polyester three-piece suit, which I wore proudly, with the shirt unbuttoned to the center of my chest. I was a pretty decent dancer. All those moves my mother had taught me in childhood came into play. Still, disco was a whole new set of body movements. The cousins helped me learn the twists and turns that I had seen in *Saturday Night Fever*.

We wandered the Mission District together, the same sidewalks that I had walked on as a child while holding my abuelita's hand. Folsom Street, Guerrero, Dolores, Capp, Van Ness Avenue, tall Victorian homes, the sun that kept the Mission bright most all days, while the rest of San Francisco was covered in fog. And all those Latinos from Mexico, Nicaragua, El Salvador, Guatemala, and Honduras. I was back in the world of my first childhood.

Odors haul us into the past faster than lightning: the intensity of *carne asada* roasting on an open grill of a food cart, the ubiquitous wafts of charred corn that ran from one street corner to another, even the smell of piss in the curb left by the homeless and the drunks, all roused in me the first years of my life. At sixteen, I could smell my childhood, this specific childhood, the one that had loved me since the moment I was born.

It was, simply put, a Latino summer. I was a teenager, and at first didn't want to have anything to do with my Salvadoran family. I was still in the throes of unrequited love. But it didn't take long. The *cariño* that the women of my childhood had shown me sprouted once more. The food, the loud Spanish conversations, the overabundance of kisses and embraces, helped me put the recent past to the side, helped me forget about my love for Anne. I dove into the ruckus of my Villatoro kin.

*

My cousin Teresa was twenty-two and had recently graduated from college. She was shorter than I by a couple of inches, and smiled all the time. She and her friend Jim took me around the city and showed me all the tourist sites—Fisherman's Wharf, Coit Tower, the Golden Gate Bridge. We rode the trolley cars and walked on the sidewalk of the curvy, serpentine Lombard Street. One day, Jim, who was one of the best dancers I had ever seen, said, "Let's go to the parade."

"Ooh, that's a great idea," Teresa said.

"What parade?" I asked.

Jim put his arms out wide and said, "Gay freedom!"

I didn't know what that meant. I don't know if I had heard the term *gay* before that day. It was a teachable moment. Jim explained it to me. Teresa stood next to him, smiling, looking into my eyes for a reaction. "You'll love it," she said. "It's the most colorful parade you'll ever see."

We made our way to Market Street and stood on the crowded sidewalk. Tourists pressed against each other to take pictures. There were children and older folks, but most of the people around us were young, closer to Teresa's age. Two men stood just in front of me. They were holding hands.

Teresa was right. The parade was a rainbow of colors. Or ten rainbows. There was a lot of skin. Some men marching down the street wore only thongs and shoes. A line of men wore Native American headdresses, others wore leather vests and pants. Women had on scant bikinis. The song "YMCA" played over the speaker of one of the floats, which was shaped like a Navy ship. As it passed, people on the streets sang along to the song that I had danced to all summer. Some broke out dancing. I wanted to join them.

A clown was walking on the edge of the parade, handing out flyers. He gave one to me. The rainbow on the page sheltered the words, "Come Out With Joy, Speak Out For Justice." There was more writing under that, about the theme, about the importance of embracing yourself for who you are.

Jim, who stood next to me, was clapping along with the music. He looked down at the paper in my hand then tapped it with his index finger. "That's what it's all about," he said.

Later that night I met Jim's boyfriend, Diego, who had come in from his job somewhere in Daly City. They hugged. They kissed. The four of us went to a restaurant in the wharf. I ate a lobster tail. Jim paid for us all.

I was happy, something that I hadn't felt in a long time. It was as though the summer in San Francisco somehow wiped away all the depressive spells I had had since as long as I could remember. The Victorian house on Capp Street was too loud and vivacious to let any sadness drag me down. And something was rising in my head. At the time I chalked it up to all the fun we were having. I didn't know that my happiness was also the beginning of the malady that would strike me soon enough, the family illness that might have played a role in the raucous ways of my relatives (how many of them carried the manic-depressive gene?).

My one shame was that I couldn't join in the Spanish conversations. I sat, uncomfortably, as my family gathered around the kitchen table and spoke in loud, mellifluous voices that were familiar and distant at the same time. But I stayed at the table, because some of the words were making sense, the words that my mother had surreptitiously taught me in Tennessee.

I look back at that summer as a glorious time. Disco. A loving, loud family. Spanish. The food—yes, the same food that Mamá had fed us in Tennessee, but more. Abuelita always had a pot of black beans on the stove. We ate pupusas, tamales, thick tortillas, picadillo. They allowed me a beer at suppertime, which was wonderful, though nothing compared to the weed that Teresa and Jim had introduced me to. Weed that loosened me up, that loosened the tight ropes of the past.

The cut on my wrist was a problem. I still hid it as best I could. I wore a wristwatch over it, and would do so for years, hiding it with the watch's face. I was a teenager, foolish to believe that no one saw it. Even though my mother had touched it, I still thought she didn't know.

But I soon learned that my Salvadoran family knew, the day I stood outside the kitchen door. My aunt Marina, Abuelita, and mother were at the table, drinking coffee. I understood enough words to figure out they were talking about me—first, because they were saying my name. Mamá said something in a rattled voice. Aunt Marina cried out, "¡Ay, no!" I heard the word *sicólogo*, and figured out what it meant by its first three syllables—a head shrink. Again, an "Ay no," though said more with disparagement than shock. That was my grandmother. She went on. I wonder how she spoke about therapy, whether it was worthless, or you couldn't trust a psychologist with your secrets, or they were just too damn expensive.

I stood at the edge of the door, sucking in shallow breaths. They kept talking. I retreated to my bedroom. A few minutes later Aunt Marina, who always wore silky, tight dresses that accentuated her voluptuous figure, with rings on half her fingers and a gold necklace with its bauble nested in her cleavage, opened my door without knocking, smiled at me, and said, "Come on *sobrino*, we're going dancing."

At the end of that summer, when Mamá and I returned to Tennessee, I knew something had changed. The sadness was gone, stripped out of me. A glorious sense of joy filled me up, unmitigated, limitless. I felt happy; not just happy, but *ebullient*. What could be wrong with that?

I returned to high school in Knoxville and lived the last two years with the Hansons. Sarah and Ben Hanson had three children, all of them in grade school. They were a loud couple who chewed on world events, such as President Jimmy Carter's recent pardoning of Vietnam War evaders. Sometimes they fought, but even though it could get as loud as it did in my own home in Rogersville, there was a different timbre to it.

Sarah and Ben were in their early forties and were deeply in love, you could tell by how they argued with each other over whatever subject was at hand. Sometimes they fought like two cats over a dead mouse, then would disappear into their bedroom. The kids knew the drill. "Mom and Dad's in there kissing and kissing," one would say.

They owned the biggest home library I had ever seen. It wasn't exactly in order, but had a disheveled look about it, with some books pushed deep into the shelves, others sticking out like loose teeth. They had magazines—the *New Yorker*, the *Atlantic*, and back copies of the *National Lampoon*. "Take whatever you want," Sarah said, "but don't dog-ear any of the books, or Ben will kick your ass." Something said light-heartedly, followed by a loud laugh. I said, "You sure?" and glanced up at one of the shelves. She looked at me, puzzled. "Of course. They're books. What else would you do with them?"

I'd had my eye on one book since the first day I'd walked into the house: a volume of *The Joy of Sex* on a high shelf, where the kids couldn't reach it.

The shelves were filled with books on history, sociology, psychology, art. Literature took up most of the space—poetry, fiction, essays. They had Shakespeare, Faulkner, the Marquis de Sade. That last one I'd never seen in Rogersville's library. I borrowed the Shakespeare and Faulkner for English classes, and kept *The Joy of Sex* in my bedroom, until Ben said, "How long you going to use that?" and winked at me.

I spent my last two years of high school there, where I started to learn more about the world. They read the newspapers, watched television news, and critiqued US policy. Then Ben started getting his news from the radio. In the mornings he'd sit in the den quietly, not wanting to be disturbed. I disturbed. "What are you listening to?" I asked.

"NPR."

"What's that?"

"National Public Radio. Shut up."

It was the day Jimmy Carter had sent helicopters into Iran to free the

American hostages. The mission, called Operation Eagle Claw, had failed. Eight American servicemen were killed. Ben shook his head and closed his eyes while listening to Bob Edwards' newscast. I'd never known anyone so concerned about world affairs.

*

It was an effervescent household, a place where I could be myself. I was happy. Too happy. I wasn't diagnosed with bipolar disorder until my thirties, but the signs had been coming on since the summer in San Francisco, when I had turned sixteen, a common age when manic depression begins.

It started with insomnia. I didn't sleep for two days. It was marvelous. I got so much work done after midnight and did it brilliantly: a science project, a midterm history paper, and studying for a Latin exam. I wasn't happy, but ecstatic. Friends asked why I talked so fast. Ideas barreled through me, too quickly for my mouth to keep up. My science project wasn't as brilliant as I imagined it to be; the teacher gave it a B-. My history teacher said that the essay rambled. It might have earned me a C. I barely passed the Latin test. I don't remember caring. I was too deep in the froth of the high to worry about such prosaic, earthly things.

But the mind can handle only so much unleashed rapture. The abyss awaited, and the exhaustion dropped me into it. That plummet still frightens me. It is the metaphor of Icarus, after he nearly touched the sun (or believed he had; no doubt that boy was bipolar). The melted wax. The feathers that slipped off the wing's wooden scaffolding. The shameful plummet into the sea. The drowning *the drowning*. Sudden depression would swamp me, especially during winter.

But oh, the mania. There's nothing like it. Sometimes, when it's at that sweet spot between equilibrium and all-out euphoria, you can rope people into your bliss. You're not sick, you're charismatic, an existential evangelical on a roll—until you go too far.

In class, I raised my hand to nearly every question the teacher posed. Mrs. Lancaster, our history teacher, had to cut me off in the middle of my rapid-fire answers. One day I danced down the hall singing the Bee Gees' "Staying Alive." Students found it amusing and some sang with me, until it went on for too long. They turned away, embarrassed, for myself as well as for watching a wannabe John Travolta disco through the school. I didn't care. The mania freed me from the pains of this life. It lifted me out of memory. Whenever on a high, I thought little of my childhood, my father's violence, Barry. The relative, who was a haunt in my brain, got lost in the joy. Ironically, the mania helped me, if not escape from the past, at least forget about it for a while.

Then there's the shift, right before the fall. Rage. It came on like clockwork. I snapped at people for no reason, machine-gunned them with a mean eloquence. The slightest thing set me off. Someone would look at me and smile. It was too much. Why? I still don't know. I don't understand the storm of mania, even though I've been in it so many times. A smile, a look, words said, words unsaid, anything could ignite the ire. I cursed like my father. Then the anger ended, and I fell-fell-fell into the morass of depression. I slept too much, spoke little at the supper table, and picked up school books as though they were millstones. I couldn't taste my food. Walking through a room was like trudging through mud.

The Hansons knew depression when they saw it, how I slumped into my chair at supper, how I turned mute, no matter how much they cajoled me with political arguments and talk about possible girlfriends. I spent weekends curled up in bed, unable to move. They were confused, and no doubt worried. I was as confused as they. Why did I have these feelings? What made me so sensitive to the world around me? Why was I happy one moment and deeply sad in the next? *Sad?* That word is an insult. The depressions were more than melancholy, though I couldn't articulate it at the time.

But with the written word, I could make out a semblance of understanding. At least, I could write down the symptoms. A girlfriend gave me my first journal. (She broke up with me soon after. I wonder if my mood swings had something to do with that.) The diary is pockmarked with suicidal ideation. As I now read some of the passages, I see that, even then, I was trying to map out what was going on in my mind.

> *It's turning winter again. I love fall, but I hate winter. I'm scared of it. I don't want to, but I think I'm going into my death depression again. You know. Thinking about death. I came home after the football game, and it just kind of hit me. I get this feeling over me that I want to die. Only this time, I don't want to kill myself. I just really wouldn't mind dying. It's hard to put down what I mean. Everything seems to be going all right, when one thing will get under my skin. Then it bothers me. It worries me. Then I start getting depressed.*
>
> *I would just like to go to sleep, and not wake up. Actually, I don't care how I die. I just wish I would.*

The irony is that after writing such entries, I felt a little better. It was as though some of the depression had cascaded from my mind and into the pen. Thus I discovered the magic that is part of writing—something powerful happens through the written word. An escape from the pain, transient as it is. So I kept writing. It became an obsession. I had a place in which to put down my shadowed thoughts and arrange them in a semblance of order.

The depressions didn't last. The mania returned, kept me afloat *and fully alive*! I did silly and dangerous things. One Friday night my friend Hank Pierce was driving us in his Ford pickup truck to the homecoming football game. I decided the night was too beautiful to stay inside the cab, opened the window, and began to crawl out. I hung onto the rearview mirror to swing myself onto the hood, while Hank took us down Interstate 40. "Get your fucking ass back in here!" He reached over and grabbed my ankle. He was a weight lifter, strong as an ox. He jerked me back in. My head hit the top of the window pane. I turned on him like a viper and tore into him with every curse word I'd heard come out of my father's mouth. It shut him up. When we parked, he turned away from me and walked into the crowd.

"Calm down," Ben had to say a few times over supper. I couldn't. Ideas and concepts ripped through me, none of which made sense. I was a whirling dervish of thoughts and words. His reprimand worked. I would get quiet, recognizing that I was acting a fool, and join in on their conversations, such as when they lambasted the Holy Catholic Church on its idiot rule about celibate priests. I called it an idiot rule too, and said that maybe the pope would change the law before I went off to seminary.

*

This news didn't surprise them, for they had seen me pray. I went through a rosary every night, on my knees, my arms laid out on the bed, the string of black beads in hand. I thumbed through them and spoke the prayers—the fifty Hail Marys separated by five Our Fathers. It took twenty minutes to get through the beads. I prayed with the same fervor that I had when living with Barry's family, but now it wasn't so based in fear. Still, it was a form of protection, a way of keeping a menacing world at bay. Once Sarah knocked. She opened the door and said, "I was wondering if you could go down to the store and—oh, my gosh, I'm sorry," as though she had caught me masturbating. "Don't let me bother you," she said, and softly closed the door.

It had been in the air, the notion that I wanted to become a priest. It tickled them both, mostly because I had talked with them about all the girls I wanted to date. Sarah said, "You'll make a good one," and smiled. Ben grinned and said, "If you make it." We were eating Kentucky Fried Chicken. He looked at me while chewing a leg and said, "Let's just see how long you can keep it in your pants." Sarah hooted with laughter.

This pissed me off and made my pledge to the priesthood even stronger. Looking back, the choice seems to have come out of nowhere. But it hadn't. Since childhood, I had been a devoted Catholic. My mother has told me about how I, at age seven, eight, would rouse her out of bed and beg her to take me to mass. Now I see that the Catholic Church, early on, had been a sanctuary from my trauma-riddled childhood. The mass gave me a structure of stability. In church, unlike at home, I knew what was coming. The predictability made for a relaxed mind. I had never known a calmer man than our pastor, Father McCain. A humble man, not one to want attention, whose homilies were said in a calm, pleasing voice.

Religion had always been a shield. Even before the year with Barry, when I had prayed for him to leave me alone, I had learned that a faith-filled life could keep chaos at bay.

When I was a kid, my parents got together regularly with a group of friends who spent Saturday nights drinking and dancing in one of their homes. They dragged their children along. While we ran around the house, playing hide and seek, the adults gathered in Harold Lyons' basement that he'd tricked out into a bar and dance floor. They drank into oblivion while we played upstairs.

One night, I decided to put on my faith in that house—not from any real concern over my soul, but to see how much my belief could control others. I must have been ten or eleven, old enough to know what I was doing. The Lyons had a Bible on hand—what Protestant southerner doesn't? While the adults partied and the other kids ran in and out of bedrooms, I sat on a recliner chair, pushed it back, read a few lines from one of the Gospels, laid the open book on my chest, and pretended to sleep.

Mrs. Lyons walked into the kitchen to grab some snacks. She was loud coming up the stairs, but she saw me, I knew this by her sudden silence. She walked back down to the basement and brought her husband up the stairs, "You've got to see this." Others followed. They gathered around the recliner. I had my eyes closed and mouth slightly open in a feigned sleep. They were mute, until Mr. Lyons said, "Look at that. He's a good boy, that one." Someone else whispered that Jesus sure was nestled deep in my heart. Mrs. Lyons shushed them. They all went back to the basement, but the music died down. They'd left the door open. I could hear them, talking, maybe about me, maybe about themselves. Someone said it was time to hit the sack. Most of them left early that night.

Though I no longer follow religion, I recognize that, in childhood up to my years in college, I did have a deep, abiding faith. The Lord was my protector. Jesus was my guide, and would remain so through my early adulthood. I am tempted to disparage all those prayers and petitions as nothing more than a trick to keep the violent at bay. It might have started with that. It may have begun with Father McCain, our calm pastor who prayed humbly, a kind man who, even when I was a child, would, after mass, shake my hand and wish my mother and me a blessed day. I believed; and today, though I have no truck with religion, I see how that belief in God kept me buoyed through the horrid times.

Priesthood had been on my mind early on. Before moving to Knoxville, I had talked with Father McCain about the vocation. He had listened to me intently, and he didn't laugh as I stumbled along, trying to express the belief that Christ was calling me to serve Him.

Finally, he smiled and said how laudable it was, that I, at age twelve, wanted to devote my life to God's people. He added that the possibility of seminary studies was a long way off, and a lot could happen in the interim. I didn't rebuke him; I was a kid. But in the Hanson house, when Ben had made his statement about keeping it in my pants, I tore into him and said he'd attend my parish someday. It didn't faze him. He nodded his head, still grinning, said, "All right," and chewed on his drumstick.

While my friends at Knoxville Catholic High School applied to colleges in our senior year, filling out loan applications and sending transcripts to various universities, all I had to do was talk to the principal about God's calling me to the vocation. Father Weber was pleased to no end. He made a phone call to a priest named Bill Mead, who was the vocational director of the diocese. Father Mead was elated, considering the paucity of priests in the southern, Protestant state of Tennessee. They did all the paperwork for me. I didn't need to worry about filling out applications for scholarships and loans, because the diocese footed the bill for their seminarians. This was good, for I had no idea what it meant to go to college. Nor could my parents have paid for the tuition. If it hadn't been for seminary, I might not have gone.

I left the Hanson home after graduation. Three months later, I traveled to Iowa, to Saint Ambrose College, where our bishop sent his seminarians for theological training.

Chapter 10

After living most of my life in the deep, rolling hills of Appalachia, the Midwest was a shock. The land was so flat, I once saw an entire train on the horizon, from engine to caboose. And corn—an ocean of corn. Who was eating it all? I thought such abundance could save entire countries from famine, until I learned that most of the corn was used to feed cows, fattening them up for slaughter.

Saint Ambrose was a small, coed college, and fit on one city block. But to me, it was a huge world. One priest, named Sam (he said we could drop the "Father" with him), took me and the other newbie seminarians around the campus. He gave us a guided tour from the dorm rooms to the library to the Union Bee community center, where they had an ample beer bar. This was the eighties; eighteen was the legal drinking age.

Many of our professors were priests. Sam, a tall, broad-shouldered man who towered above us all, taught sacramental theology. Father Joe Murphy, much shorter than Sam and who grew his auburn hair long, nearly to his shoulders, was a systematic theologian. Father Francis Bearden, a bookish fellow with glasses who always had a tome in hand, taught scripture and ignited in me a love for the Bible, which I still hold close—not as a religious text, but a literary one. We also had lay professors, but the seminarians tended to cluster around the clerics.

Saint Ambrose was the college where our bishop had attended, decades before, when it was just a seminary. All-male. But with the dearth of men being called to the vocation, the college, to keep afloat, went coed. We seminarians were the minority at the school and were housed in one building in the middle of the campus. The rest of the college was made up of lay students, men and women who filled the other dorm rooms, who majored in sociology, business, psychology, art, mathematics, like in any other college. We took classes along with them, mixed with them, partied with them. It didn't take long: several seminarians started to lose their call to priesthood. Out of the fifteen seminarians in my class, only one would get ordained. The rest fell in love.

We learned a sophisticated theology, one that followed a certain logic. You begin with Christ's resurrection and build on that, though sometimes it felt like the priests dutifully referred to that focus of the Christian faith then rushed to the real subjects they wanted to cover: Justice. The plight of the poor. The horror of possible nuclear annihilation. The wars in Central America that the US government funded. Earthly things all. In many classes, God was hardly mentioned.

And *blasphemy*. That wasn't part of the curriculum, but whenever the seminarians and the priests gathered together for drinks in Father Murphy's apartment, we students sat back and listened, as though happy hour were a continuation of classes. With drinks in hand, our professors said things that no priest dared utter from the pulpit. They spoke of Jesus' manhood. Though He was the son of God, He also was completely human and, as Sam once said, "probably had an erection from time to time." Such titillation! Father Murphy took on the virgin birth: The early Church Fathers had written up the story several decades after Jesus was born. "They stole it from the Greeks!" Father Murphy said. "Leda and the Swan! Zeus saw Leda, fell in love, turned into a swan, and raped her. She gave birth to Helen, which launched the Greek civilization." He could get quite animated. "See it? See it? With Mary, scripture says that the Holy Spirit came upon her like a dove. In both stories, the bird did it." Then he dared to say what must not be said to the laity, that it was a story, a myth, and that God could have easily made the miracle happen through Joseph's own seed.

I learned about ethics there, learned what it meant to be a man of Christ (or as Father Bearden put it, to be more inclusive of nonbelievers, "Simply a good man."). We took psychology classes, where I began to understand, on an academic, cerebral level, the mental pathologies in my family. In philosophy classes, we read the atheists, from Epicurus to Diderot to Bertrand Russell. Those philosophers challenged our faith. That was the idea: question everything. Even your own beliefs.

*

El Salvador was in the news nearly every night. A war had broken out there, one fomented by President Ronald Reagan in his hell-bent attempt to wipe communism out of the Americas. There was a corrupt government and military, and a guerrilla force called the FMLN that, as Sam put it, "is fighting for the people." For years, Reagan had sent money to the Salvadoran government, who handed it over to the military, who practiced tactics taught to them by the CIA: Death squads. Torture. Disappearance. The priests railed against Reagan. Father Murphy would shake his glass of scotch at the television without spilling a drop and rip into old Ronald right and left. Sam had to calm him down from time to time, usually with a "Shut the hell up Joe, I can't hear a word Dan Rather's saying."

El Salvador. I knew nothing of what was going on there. The more we watched the news, and the more the professors railed against US policy, the more I squirmed. These men knew more about my mother's home country than I did. One night, during his rants, Father Murphy turned and looked at us seminarians. He saw us for what we were: awestruck students who lapped up everything the priests said, which he didn't like. He was a professor to the bone, and preferred participation. He must have seen me squirm. "What about you?" he asked. "What do you think about the situation in El Salvador?"

I was stuck. I still couldn't distinguish between the Salvadoran guerrilla group the FMLN and the US-backed death squads that murdered civilians. I didn't understand US policy, and had not, until those nights, given much thought to our president. I started to mumble, and somewhere in that mumble I mentioned that my mother was from El Salvador.

All the priests and the seminarians turned to me. Father Murphy said, "You're kidding! Really? That's wonderful!" He turned to the others and said that we had a bona fide Central American in our midst. I bathed in the attention, until Father Murphy, who had spent a year working in Bolivia when he was a young man, said something akin to "Entonces tú sabes lo que pasa allá, ¿sí?" Actually, I have no idea what he said.

I muttered, "I'm not too good with . . . I can't speak Spanish."

Father Murphy must have seen it in my eyes: the confused, vexing embarrassment that a young Latino feels when called out on his ignorance of his own culture. He understood. His look softened. He said, "Oh. Well, that's all right." He patted my shoulder, turned away from my shame and back to Dan Rather's reporting.

Those were effervescent years. But they didn't quell the illness, which was growing. The episodes began to follow a certain pattern. According to my journals, I became more manic during the spring and depressed in winter. It came down hard on me in December of my freshman year. I had spent two days trying to figure out what the hell was going on inside me. Everywhere I turned, there was an invisible sheen of anguish. It was the bipolar; but the manic depression also came on hard whenever the past nipped at me, which it did, a lot, in winter. In weak moments, the relative would shoot through me like an icepick through the skull.

I've also been diagnosed with seasonal affective disorder, which many times comes with the bipolar package. High in the spring, low in the winter. That winter was a mix of both. I was depressed, but didn't sleep. The erratic mood swings set off the memories, or the broken-glass echo of the memories. I tried my best not to dwell on all that had happened in childhood: a predator relative, a violent father, a sadistic, homophobic teenager. It was the relative who haunted me the most. I tried to be all manly about it, saying to myself, *That shit happened, but it's in the past. Nothing but now and the future for me.* Life was a timeline, and the more I traveled on that line, the further away I would be from what he had done to me. He would, I believed, shrink and disappear, like a car wreck caught in a rearview mirror. All I needed was time to take me away from the past.

But two days without sleep pulled me inward so deeply, with no explanation, no rhyme or reason to it. Maybe I'd gotten stressed with school work (stress can ignite mental illness and PTSD). I don't know. I just remember taking my pocket knife and walking into the catacombs of the church.

This was in the basement. A series of mini-altars was built into the granite walls, one next to the other, where priests long ago celebrated daily mass to themselves. Now it was just a shadowy place where few people visited. There was an air of a haunting about it. It was one of my favorite places on campus, where I could be alone; where I could pray.

I prayed the night I took my knife down there. I kneeled before one of the little altars, the blade clasped in my hands, shaking with the illness and the abuse. There was something inside, a demon, Satan himself, wriggling, ready to burst through my skin. I just needed to cut myself to let him out. I imagined my friends finding me down there, bled out. I imagined a funeral outside of holy church property, in Dante's forest of suicides. I placed the blade on my wrist, pressed down, let a tiny trickle of blood pop out around the metal and stopped. The pain made me hesitate. But if I just pulled harder and faster than I had pulled in high school, and if I could get both wrists open, it would be over.

I didn't. I made my way back upstairs and stayed in my room until the next morning. I couldn't sleep. The demon hadn't gone away. Again, I considered the knife.

There was a special mass that afternoon, the celebration of Saint Ambrose, whom the college was named after. The bishop was going to be the main celebrant, with four or five priests standing alongside him, including our professors. I was exhausted. And the bishop was boring as hell. I sat alone in a back pew. My head bobbed. I fell asleep and woke to a lot of slobber on my shirt.

Just like that, it was gone—the inner, compacted pain that pushed against my skin, the desire to die. The sudden nap had somehow stripped it all away. I now think that the sleep, after days without it, had rebooted my brain's chemicals. But at the moment I believed the Holy Spirit had entered my mind and chased the demon out. I was happy, suddenly rested. I didn't question the incident, didn't analyze it. It was clear the holy mass had saved my life. God, finally, must have intervened.

*

There were fewer moments of suicidal ideation, fewer drops into sudden depression. No more knives in the catacombs. I learned a daily pattern, an order that helped keep my head on straight. Communal prayers in the morning, classes, studying, exercise, attending late afternoon mass with my fellow seminarians, followed by what was becoming nightly medicine: scotch.

The exercise surprised me. I had never been one for athletics, but one day, on a whim, I decided to go running. It didn't take long to see that jogging cleared my head. For hours after the run, I would feel calmer. Supposedly, the aerobics kicks up the serotonin in your brain, the mind-wash that brings on a certain tranquility.

But exercise, staying busy, and drinking didn't cure me. I still struggled with the moods. Journal writing became more important than ever. In the mornings, before matins prayers, I rose early to write a page or two in the diary. I didn't write directly about the relative, but those pages reveal the ongoing struggle to cleave the past from the present.

After a while, I picked up on a fledgling desire from high school—writing poetry. I discovered that pain can be turned into verse, and the very act of writing can both churn and replenish the mind. As time passed, I rose earlier from bed, before sunrise, so as to spend more time on the poems. Though there was still a shaky feel to the days, writing poetry helped me forge ahead.

Chapter 11

For a while, life was stable. But the past leaks into the present. It always will, especially when something or someone comes around and rattles it. It was Father Mead who did it, our vocational director back in Tennessee. The priest not only roused the rapes from childhood; he and the relative have been linked together in my mind ever since 1981. Only recently, after years of pondering and therapy and writing about it in my journals, have I been able to separate them from each other. Still, I can't dwell on the priest for too long. Writing about him here is almost as difficult as writing about the relative. The difference is, Father Mead, because of me, got caught. Sometimes I've wondered if, had I pushed more, he might have gone to jail.

That's a foolish notion. This was the 1980s, long before the corruption of the Catholic Church's hiding of predatory priests came into the public eye. Later I learned that before I came along, it was already known amongst a few leaders in the diocese that Father Mead "had a problem." But they had done or said nothing about it.

Decades have passed, but I still can see myself, the nineteen-year-old, in that apartment, alone with Father Mead, in a parish rectory on a Sunday night. I was going home for the winter holidays and had gotten a ride from one of the other Tennessee seminarians to Nashville. From there, I would catch a Greyhound bus to Rogersville the next morning.

Father Mead had invited me to spend the night in the rectory. There, he sniffed me out. I don't recall exactly how it began. Maybe it was because he was a popular priest among the seminarians, and I wanted to be in that group. I ended up telling him about parts of my past, though I never mentioned the relative; that was too much to unleash. He listened, as though hearing my confession. I don't remember all I said, except for my father's alcoholism and his meanness. It was enough to make me break down and cry. He listened; he was so empathetic, or appeared to be.

He was the principal of a Catholic high school and vocation director for all the seminarians. A handsome man—there was a bit of Brad Pitt in his features. He was on the quiet side, and had that Tennessee good-old-boy demeanor about him. But now, he was on the hunt.

His strategy on me was strange, and ham-fisted. He sat back on a sofa, kicked his feet up onto the coffee table, drank his cognac, and said, "You know, I feel like I could tell you anything. It's like you're already a priest." He went on for a while about my maturity, that I was so much more ahead of all the other seminarians. He said he felt like he was going to confession with me. I bathed in the praise, but there was something ominous about it, that he was going to tell me a story that no one could ever know about, something that I could not repeat to anyone. I was right. He told me everything.

He had had sex with one of the sophomores at the high school. He went into detail, how the boy had seduced him, how they had been in this very apartment when they did it. How Father Mead was the one to say to the boy, "This isn't right, we shouldn't do this," and the boy said, "Come on, Father, how can something that feels so right be wrong?"

My antennae started to crackle. That dialogue just didn't sound right. But he kept going. They had "made love" several times, until the day the boy got in a fight with another student and was dragged to the principal's office. His parents were there. The boy sat in a center chair. Father Mead tremulously said to the parents that this sort of conduct wouldn't do, and something had to be done about it. Supposedly the boy smiled, chuckled, and said, "I don't think you're going to do a *thing* about it."

Mead paused and took a sip of cognac.

"What happened?" I asked.

"I had to have him sent off to juvie." Mead explained: He himself was too important a man in the diocese, and if word of his "affair" with the boy got out, it could shake the entire Tennessee Catholic community to its knees. He asked if I wanted another drink. I declined.

After that, he got to work touching me every chance he could. I was wearing a T-shirt and an old pair of gym shorts as pajamas. He sat next to me, grabbed my thigh—gripped it, really—rubbed it up and down, getting closer to the groin with each slide. I said I had to use the bathroom and got up. He slapped my buttocks. I stayed in the bathroom until he said, "You all right? I'd like to take a shower." I came back into the den. He put a movie in his Beta machine, *Star Wars*. He took his bath. I sat and watched the film and saw nothing. He returned, with only a towel around his waist. "Come here," he said, with such a warm smile. I stood. He walked to me, put his face hardly six inches from mine, said that I was a wonderful listener, that he could imagine me hearing many a confession in just a few years, "when you become one of us." Then he called out my name and said I was so wonderful, more mature than the rest of the seminarians, more a man than any of them.

He flicked apart the half-knot of the towel. It fell to the floor. He took my head in his hands, pulled me to him and kissed me, hard, his tongue pressing against my tightly closed lips. I froze. Every single muscle in my body tightened. He must have felt the shiver run through me, because he finally pulled away, left the towel on the floor, and walked back to the bathroom.

He didn't do anything after that. But it was enough. I felt trapped, as though Mead had put me in a cage. He didn't say, *Don't tell anybody*; it didn't need to be said. He was a man with ecclesial power. I was a seminarian. My silence was a given.

I spent that winter vacation with my mother in Rogersville. It was quiet, and I needed it. I stayed in bed for days, reading Steinbeck's *East of Eden*. At midnight, I'd jog under the black, star-glistening sky of my home town, where I listened to my breath, listened to the crunch of snow under my shoes, felt the bite of cold on my face, and got to work trying to block Mead out of my mind.

I couldn't. He hadn't gotten any further than the kiss. But his story, and his moves on me, his power over me—yes, I was afraid, so afraid. He had control. I knew no one would believe me. At the time, I didn't connect it with the relative of childhood. All I knew was a priest had come on to me. A priest who had told me a story that was supposed to keep my mouth shut. But he couldn't send me to juvie; I was a man, all of nineteen years old. What could he do to me? One logical conclusion: he could have me kicked out of the seminary. But there was more, I believed. For some reason, I imagined going to jail, for slander. He would have me arrested for publicly staining his name. And the other priests in my life, the ones whom I had come to love—would they turn on me? Would they believe me? It felt like freshman year in high school, when I was too afraid to speak to anyone about Barry's sadism. All of this was a trap, a metal box that was squeezing me in.

It squeezed too much. It set off something in me, a realization: I hated being trapped.

The fear began to morph into anger. Mead had set off the mania. What priest would take a high school sophomore to bed? It made no sense. He was, I figured, an anomaly, someone whom the other priests would look upon with disdain. Maybe they'd kick him out. Was that possible? Once a priest, always a priest. It all swirled in me, until the mania reached that certain place between equilibrium and all-out madness. That sweet spot before the fall, the place where the sickness can make a man do outrageous things, like tell on an authority.

On one midnight jog, I left the road, ran into some nearby woods and yelled so hard my throat ached. I paced, with my hands on my hips. Breaths billowed out of me. In the forest, the anger became stronger than the fear. It was pure, solid, unsullied by any other emotion. Clarity.

After winter break, I told the whole story to Fathers Murphy, Sam, and Bearden. They listened. Father Murphy, after I had finished, fell back in his chair, swept his fingers through his long, thick hair, and said, "Oh, oh my gosh." The other two said nothing. It was a horrid silence. I twitched with fear.

Finally, Sam said, "Something's got to be done." He assured me that they would take care of it.

They did, in the old-fashioned, clerically hermetic way: it was an in-house problem, something that they didn't want to report to anyone outside the confines of the priesthood. A week passed. Sam smiled and said to me, "Don't worry. I've been in contact with your diocese. It's been taken care of. He won't bother you again."

That was enough. I felt safe. Only later did I learn how they took care of it: Sam had called our bishop in Tennessee. The bishop took Mead out of the high school and gave him another job: dean of the diocese, which was a much more powerful position than that of being a principal. I still shook from it all, but felt better. My beloved priests hadn't turned on me, but had protected me. I started to loosen up, with Sam's promise of Mead leaving me in peace.

He didn't leave me in peace. Mead knew that I had told. He made a trip to Iowa. He said he was visiting to check in on his seminarians. But I knew that he was there to see me. I avoided him, skittering around the college like a hunted rabbit. He kept tracking me down. He passed by classrooms and looked in to find me. I avoided mass, knowing that my professor priests, who knew what he had done, had invited him to concelebrate. I didn't attend, but I watched from the edge of a door to the side of the sacristy. There they were, all four of them around the altar, as though nothing had happened. At the sign of peace, they hugged one another.

I was frightened. But it was rising, once again, and when I think about that rise, I nearly give thanks for the bipolar in me. Anger. Fury. Something that had been in me all along; something that had been in my family for generations. But this anger, as wild as it could become, was focused. Then the relative *did* come to mind, seemingly for the first time. So did Barry. Both had trapped me. Now, I would do everything I could to break out of the cage, for the first time.

It happened on the last day of his visit. Mead stood at my dorm room door, waiting for me to return from class. I was at the far end of the hall. I ducked behind a corner and thought, *Just wait for him to leave*, followed by, *Fuck that shit*.

I stormed down the hallway. He turned and smiled at me. "Oh, I was just looking for you. There's something I want to talk to you about."

I walked faster, trembling, caught between utter fear and rage. He was still talking, saying something about how I had misunderstood everything. I reached the door, took out my key with one hand, raised my index finger of the other to his face and growled, "Don't ever come near me again." I said more. Now, *he* shook. I didn't stop. I cursed him, and finally said, "You leave me the fuck alone!" It was an unbridled anger; I barely kept it contained within my quaking body. I walked into my room and slammed the door closed.

Inside the room, I shook. I had taken on an authority. But it had worked. I didn't know then what the relative had confessed to me years later, how I had screamed, *Quit it! It hurts!* All I knew was, my adult voice had put a priest at bay.

Mead returned to Tennessee. A week later he called me. "Listen, I think you misunderstood me but if I've hurt you in any way please know I'm sorry I hope you can forgive me but there's no reason to worry about it anymore and you don't need to tell anybody else anything, it's all over." He hung up.

I heard he stayed in the priesthood for a few more years. Then the past caught up with him. Two decades later, the boy he had raped in the high school spoke publicly about what had happened. It became a scandal. The Tennessee newspapers were all over it. Mead's hidden sins became public knowledge.

I left the seminary. The three priests didn't argue, as though knowing better. Instead, they took care of me. They knew I couldn't afford college, and that I'd have to return to Tennessee, probably without ever graduating from any university. They didn't want that for me. And I still believe that, because the goodness they bestowed upon me was great. Father Murphy gave me a job as a part-time secretary of the Theology Department. Sam made me the editor of the school yearbook, which meant my tuition was waived. Bearden moved out of his home and gave it to me to house-sit while he moved to a parish just outside of town. I had free room and board for the rest of my college years.

Through the years I have deconstructed all that goodness in order to look at its underbelly. They weren't just taking care of me. Their acts of kindness were also hush money. They were good men who taught about social justice. But they were enclosed within the culture of priesthood, where they had learned to keep certain incidents under cover. This saddens me; for I loved those men, and still love them for all they had taught me.

But now I recognize that they were of their time, when predator priests were hidden by the church. They were part of the conspiracy. It hurts to dwell on that.

That time was a turning point. Anger had freed me from the cage. All those classes on social justice had a lot to do with it: the cry of the poor, the demand for radical social change, the need for revolution. But it was more than that. It was, I believe, in part due to the illness. Though I didn't recognize it at the time, my mother's rage was coming out of me. It was becoming part of my voice.

I suppose that we all, after enough years have passed, look back to search for patterns, to see a road that inevitably brought us to where we are now. We believe that life is a timeline of events. One experience leads to another; one decision marks the upcoming trail. Some will take it a step further: "It was meant to be," or some other phrase that evokes the notion of Fate. There's a small leap from that to the idea of an intervening God. I understand this; I had begged for God's intervention throughout my childhood. It never happened, so I had turned on myself, blamed myself. I had prayed to God, not so much for Him to intercede, but to give me strength to handle the attacks. This carried me for a long while. Now I see that those prayers were desperate pep talks to myself.

But the three events—the relative, Barry, Mead—were not my decisions, not my choices. It would take decades for me to grasp this, to believe it. Before, I would wonder what it was about me that attracted such men to do what they did. Since then I've learned that trauma in childhood can set the child up for more trauma in the future. I've wondered if both Barry and Mead could smell out the damaged goods that the relative had left in me.

This was the pattern I saw, for much of my life: my first two decades were a timeline of abuse. The relative-Barry-Mead; I was trapped into that mode of thinking. That definition, the pattern I had created in my head, locked me down. I could see no more than the diabolical. It wasn't until I confronted Mead that I broke the chain.

Because *I* had chosen. I had made the decision—sudden, enraged, honed—to take him on. And he backed down. Yes, he got away; and yes, the one institution that had buoyed me through my childhood and adolescence had betrayed me. But I had won a battle. I had spoken. I had, in cursing him out, screamed.

Still, the pattern of the three attacks grafted itself to my synapses, most especially the rapes of childhood. It had played a role in shaping my five-year-old brain, and no doubt exacerbated the bipolar (I have wondered, had the rapes not happened, if I would suffer from manic depression at all). Yet now I understand the use of the term *survivor*. Since the beginning, my little brain was desperately making choices to try to survive. It learned how to duck and cover, how to be obsequious to pacify others' actions, how to use faith as a shield. Finally, it learned to yell.

But the sequence of attacks at times overwhelmed me (and overwhelms me still). The problem was, I saw only one trajectory, and I couldn't see, in the shadow of that trajectory, another pattern that had come along with me on the same path, one that was a bit random, but now, in recollection, seems purposeful, meaningful. It's simple and, in my mind, elegant: childhood rape followed by the trip to El Salvador. San Francisco after teenage suicidal depression. My Latino roots were always there, hidden for the most part. The excursions to the Central American worlds after each attack now hold great meaning for me. After Mead's attempt, El Salvador would make yet one more appearance. The first two trips to my Latino roots, along with my childhood in San Francisco, were sparks against the kindling. Then there was another passage—this time to Mexico—that would set the kindling to burst into a bonfire.

Before that trip, however, something else would come along and play a role in my survival. Or better said, my happiness. A simple thing; a kiss.

Chapter 12

Michelle Menster and I had met in Father Murphy's social justice class while I was still in the seminary. She was a sociology major, with a minor in theology. We became friendly, though I was still in my celibacy phase and taking it seriously. It didn't matter how attractive a woman was to me, I had to wrestle with my desires in order to be faithful to my calling.

Michelle was lovely—blonde hair, hazel eyes. Her glasses gave her that certain librarian look, which worked on me all the more. I was, as Ben had said to me when I lived with his family, doing my best to keep it in my pants. But I was a seminarian, deep into my studies. Besides, I knew instinctively that I wouldn't have a chance with her. But we hung out more with each other, spent time after class talking in the hallways and walking across campus to the cafeteria, where we ate lunch together, just the two of us.

Michelle had spent the previous summer working as a volunteer with the elderly in South Dakota, through a program sponsored by Franciscan nuns. It had been her first time away from home and had changed her life. She knew she wanted to spend more time traveling, working in faraway places. She had considered missionary work in foreign countries. The Liberation Theology classes made her commitment stronger. And she was an artist, though a little shy about it. After much cajoling on my part, she let me see some of her work. They were very good—precise, clear. She showed me a drawing she had made of one of the Franciscans in a prayerful pose. The nun's veil spread back from her head like a cape.

I was smitten.

I decided to join choir, because Michelle was there. I was a pretty good tenor. They even had me do a couple of solos, which I belted out with a religious, manic-driven fervor, thankfully on-key.

Michelle volunteered in the college's day care center, where professors and staff left their children while they worked. I suddenly became interested in child development, and joined her. There might have been fifteen children running around in the basement of one of the classroom buildings. One kid with red hair and freckles named Herbert fell on the carpeted floor. He cried, as much out of embarrassment as the rug burn. Michelle helped him up, "Come here, honey, it's okay, you just stay here until it stops hurting." Herbert stood in front of her, sniffling, drying his eyes with his shirt sleeve. He was looking out at the other kids. Michelle placed her hands on his shoulders. At one point, he leaned his head back against Michelle's thin tummy and let it rest there, and I thought, *Oh God if only I were Herbert.*

We left the day care center and, as had become our habit, walked to her car. She lived off campus. I don't know what we talked about, all I remember is her saying, "Would you like to come over for dinner?"

"Sure."

She smiled. "Let me just make a phone call."

She used the pay phone next to one of the dorm buildings. I stood behind her. She said, and I hear it so clearly now, as it meant a sign of hope, "Mom, I'll just eat one less taco."

She hung up, turned, and smiled at me. "We're having tacos." Then she cringed slightly. "I'm sure they're not like what your mother makes." (She knew about my Latino roots.)

We got into her car and drove away from the campus. She lived a couple of miles from the college. I met her whole family—all eight of them. The Mensters had six kids, ranging from nineteen years old to one. Michelle was the oldest. We sat around the dining table (they had to scrunch me in). Mr. Menster made drinks. He handed me a scotch. It was the family dynamic that impressed me. Her parents were very involved in their children's lives. Mrs. Menster, a stay-at-home mom, placed the hard-shell tacos on the table. She had made plenty for us all. Mr. Menster kept his children engaged by asking about their days, their studies, the high school football game that was coming up the following Friday. The conversation was louder than any other family I had lived with, and it was, as my mother would have said to me, *alegre,* joyful.

After the meal, as some of the other kids helped their mother clean up, Michelle and I sat and chatted. Maria, her youngest sibling—one year old—was sitting atop the dining room table. I put my arms out slightly and talked with her, coaxing her to come my way. She looked at me as though I were some idiot thing, then scooted over to Michelle and crawled into her lap. I said, "She's a sweety."

"Do you like kids?" Michelle asked, a bit abruptly.

I didn't know if I did; I'd never given the question any thought. So I said, "Oh yeah."

"But, you won't be able to have any, you know, as a priest."

I kept my eyes on Maria. Something clicked. I said, "Well, that's up in the air now."

"Really?"

"Oh, I don't know. Maybe."

I stumbled along. I don't remember all I said. But I do, clearly, remember what she said, "Would you like another drink?"

She drove me back to campus. I made it in time for evening prayers. I sat there, mumbling along, thinking about nothing but the supper with the Mensters. It was becoming too much. I was still a seminarian, but now I was struggling with celibacy more than I ever had in the two years of theological training. For the first two weeks of February, I wandered from classroom to church to the cafeteria in a fog. I threw up in the mornings, and started to miss community prayers.

On February 18 of that year, after choir practice, I walked Michelle to her car. It was terribly cold, I said, and there was ice on the parking lot, I wouldn't want her to fall. It was so lame. It was she, a homegrown Iowan who had known the worst of winters, who helped me over the ice, holding my forearm to keep me steady.

We walked to her car. It was a huge, old LTD. I trembled from the cold. I trembled from the choice, a strategy that had no real structure, just momentum. But the chance was slipping away. She stuck the key into the door. I would lose her. I touched her shoulders and turned her to me. She looked confused. I let her go, stuck my hands in my pockets, pulled them out and started gesticulating and chattering like a squirrel. It tumbled out of me, "I have never met anyone as interesting as you."

She smiled, but she still wasn't sure. She raised one hand, made it into a fist, popped my upper arm—like a buddy—and said, "Well, good luck on your English test tomorrow." My guts did things guts ought not do—twist until they're on the edge of ripping.

There was no thought to it, no planning. I said, "I can think of nothing, nor no one, but you." I kissed her.

She grabbed my arms to steady herself. It was a long kiss. I still taste it now, still feel the cold of that night and the warmth of her lips. We finally pulled away from each other for breath. But I only breathed once and shot into "I'm leaving the seminary! I don't have the calling! I thought I did, but really, no no not at all!"

She listened. Once I slowed down, she patted my chest with her palms. "Let's talk tomorrow," she said. This time, she kissed me. We held it for a long while. I'm sure it was sloppy, but in memory it is perfect.

We came up for air again and I asked, "When tomorrow?" I didn't give her a chance to answer, "Let me take you out. Supper. We'll go to supper. You want to go out for supper?" She said yes. She got in the car, started it, smiled at me through the window, and drove off. There she went, an Iowan, practiced in the ways of ice and cold, someone who knows how to drive on frozen roads, but not that night. The car's back end swished in a light fish-tail.

I announced my departure from seminary. None of the priests were surprised. That's when they gave me the house, the secretarial job, and the free tuition. What they didn't know was that, in handing me what was basically hush money, they were also building for my new girlfriend and me a love nest, where we could play house. I could stay in college because of them. I could stay with Michelle.

She and I took great advantage of Father Bearden's home. I cooked, we ate, sometimes just the two of us, other nights with friends, some of whom had left the seminary as well to follow love. They brought their new mates with them, men and women both. Then our friends would leave. We had the entire house to ourselves, for two years. I felt whole. We were very different—I the dance-on-the-edge, flamboyant, exuberant romantic, she the down-to-earth, practical woman who didn't rely on histrionics to show her love. We took more social justice classes together and learned more about the struggles in Central America.

I look back and see it as an effervescent time, though my journals reveal that it wasn't all joy. Depression still would make its visits, especially in winter. In manic times, I railed loud and long against Ronald Reagan. But it wasn't as bad as before. Michelle's very personality ballasted me. She was a rock of homeostasis. I forgot about Mead and left the seminary with no regrets. The past was just that—past. All of it, all the way back to my fifth year, up to the incident with Mead. I was so caught up in my new life, the predators hardly ever came to mind.

*

It was in Bearden's house where I first heard *Adagio for Strings*. I had made coffee and was ready to sit down at the desk and write. It was an early Saturday morning. I was alone, and wanted to be; for the mornings of solitude had become a sacred time.

It was autumn. I had been living in the house for about six months. All was settled. I was having fewer mood swings than before. There was an order to my days: mornings alone to write, followed by classes, exercise, and now, spending the evenings with Michelle. The order kept me in a certain equilibrium.

That Saturday morning, I turned on the radio to the local classical music station, right when the announcer said, "And now, for your listening pleasure, the *Adagio for Strings* by Samuel Barber." I was already working before the first note hit. *Hit* isn't the right word. The first touch of a bow on a string started it, a slip of notes that slowly rose. I didn't start feeling it until about two minutes in. It was strange; the music had me stop banging the keys of my old manual Royal. I sat there and listened to the gradual rise of the strings, how they slipped, one over the other, in a perpetual climb.

It's a long piece, about nine minutes. There is a romantic feel about it, how it rises from those first notes, how other stringed instruments blend into the piece as it lifts. I consider that moment. It is with me again. I am there, in Father Bearden's house, with coffee in hand, a typewriter before me, a radio playing. Nothing else is important, only this piece of music that has gently swallowed me. I lift with the notes. It builds, like a soul being pleased. Sexual and more—it rises and digs into me, carries me with it, and easily lifts me into a gradual, thickening ecstasy that I have felt before. Not the rage; not the self-destructive behavior; just the rise itself, pure. A mania is coming on, but it lifts within the soft, firm notes of the *Adagio*. I feel protected, feel that I can allow it, as though I could ever stop it. It lifts me like a spirit to the heavens, stars and lightning. It builds, builds; it is nearly excruciating. My mind rises, as though pressing against the top of my skull. How far can those strings reach upward? Is there no ceiling to the ebullience I am feeling? The music reaches a peak, the strings all coming together in a final push to the top. Then it ends. Sudden silence.

I fall into the silence. I lift my arms and sail through it, dropping fast, knowing I will hit the earth and not caring. It is a long plummet, like the Devil dropping from heaven into the hole of Hell. And I don't care. I only feel the drop, the sudden plunge into what I know so well.

The silence lasts for ten full seconds, as though the piece were over. But it's not over. Before I slam against the earth, the music begins again, a low sweep of it, and catches me. It cradles me. It shepherds me into a vast pasture of music, slow, soft. I have experienced a musical version of my own illness.

I wept, heaving with tears. I couldn't control my shallow breathing, couldn't get up from the chair. The coffee grew cold. Before the announcer came on again, I clicked off the radio, not wanting any other piece of music to ruin what I had just gone through. An aesthetic manic-depressive episode. I was useless for the rest of the day.

In memory, it seems to come out of the blue, that the experience was born in a vacuum. But it wasn't. I was in a good place in life. A girlfriend, a home, school, the typewriter, friends. And I was safe, with Father Mead shivering in Tennessee for getting caught. He was far away. He rarely came to mind. There had been a certain tranquility in the air when the *Adagio* came along. It was as though the music were saying, *You're safe now*. Even after it was over, the piece swamped me in its echo. I felt both cleansed and in pain, like a man who's held a grip on a stone for protection for so long, once the threat has passed, he lets it go, and the letting go itself hurts. The fingers ache from so much clutching. The rock falls. The man stands there, safe, exhausted. Then a piece of music comes along and shakes him to the bones.

I'm not saying that you have to have a mental illness to fully enjoy the *Adagio for Strings*. I'm sure many a person has wept while listening to it. But how many of us have felt their soul being lifted maniacally into the heavens, only to have it drop through emptiness before being caught in the next movement of music? For nine minutes I felt the ecstasy. Afterwards, the weariness came on from holding too much in. Again, I couldn't articulate it, couldn't connect the music with all those burdens. It was the sweeping up of my soul that mattered on that Saturday morning, and the cleansing tears, and the exhaustion, that allowed for a semblance of peace to nest in me.

Chapter 13

It was a restful time; but I was not always at rest, though I tried to be. Manic depression tends to get worse as time goes on, especially if not treated—and especially when it's yoked with PTSD. It took more effort to stay on an even keel, to not feel unhelmed. Two years had passed since Michelle and I had met. Graduation was coming soon. I was planning to go to graduate school. It was a stressful time. Life started to lose its sense of stability.

I was alone the day it happened. It was an afternoon. I had woken in a quandary of moods—mostly anxiety. Why, I had no idea, and I didn't understand that the far past had come to visit on its own. Nothing had happened as far as I can remember to rouse it. It came out of nowhere, or so it seems now. It was the same horror that had taken me into the catacombs with a knife in freshman year.

That day was pure hell. I couldn't concentrate in classes. I didn't write. I made a sandwich, but it had no taste. I took my daily jog, but it wasn't working; the moment I stopped, that strange anguish came on again. I showered, dressed, then paced through the house from kitchen to bedroom to living room. It felt like someone was in the house with me. I hit my forehead with my palms, trying to bang the tremors out of my skull. It was happening on its own, and I couldn't control it. And that presence in the room; who was it? *What's going on? Why am I feeling this?* It was pure desperation, jagged, like broken glass lifting and slicing through my brain. Rage was building along with it, unbound, looking for a target. But there was no target, until Michelle came to the door.

It was then when she saw, for the first time, the Jekyll-Hyde part of the disease, made worse by the trauma. For the trauma was in the room.

Again, it was the vortex: the illness swirled together with the violence of childhood. The image of the relative shot through my skull. I saw him in jagged, lightning moments.

Michelle walked in, smiled at me, but saw my face—I picture it contorted, bent and reshaped by the illness—and stopped. "Honey? Are you all right?" I left her at the door, walked into the kitchen, leaned against the countertop, then ran back out into the den. I talked, about what, I don't know. It came out of me in a mean staccato. Then I turned to her—I turned *on* her.

"Where have you been?" I said. She said nothing. "WHERE have you BEEN GODDAMMIT?" I railed on, cursed her for her absence, that she should have been there—why, I don't know. She backed up against the front door, watching me as I paced, then, every few seconds, turned to her with what I'm sure looked like murder in my eyes. I screamed, then slammed the bottom of my palm against the wall, over and again.

The pain in my hand helped calm me down. I slowly slipped from Hyde back into Jekyll. I could feel the muscles in my face lax. I looked at her. *Oh no, oh no—I will lose her.* She shivered. Her arms were tight against her chest. I apologized, said I didn't know what was going on, but I wasn't feeling well. The remorse, the shame barreled through me, and I did what I thought would make it all right: I took her in my arms, whispered into her ear, held her tight. She still quaked. I kept apologizing, and asked her to lie down with me on the couch. There, I massaged her scalp and whispered promises. She lay there with me, all her muscles tight, her mouth shut, her jaw locked in fear. I promised never to do it again. I held onto her, locked her in that embrace. Though it was early afternoon, I proposed that we have a drink. She stayed. I made supper. In my mind, all was back to normal. But she ate little, and said less.

This is the godawful part of the disease. When on a rage, it's difficult for a witness to distinguish, to separate, the person from the illness. Even for those who have been educated about manic depression, it is near impossible to separate the two. The fury *is* the man.

I had been angry before, but this was too much. It was wrong, and I told myself so. The next day, much calmer, I again apologized and said it wouldn't happen again. She said nothing. But I could see it in her eyes; she was considering.

She didn't leave me. I kept to my word. The explosion had released some of the pressure in my brain. I still tweaked with moments of anger and fear, though I had no more violent blowups that year. But I had done damage, and knew it.

We went on with our lives and didn't speak of the incident. We settled back into our relationship. We ate with friends, studied together, spent the evenings together into the early mornings. Michelle's parents weren't surprised at all when I asked for their daughter's hand. We married five days after graduation.

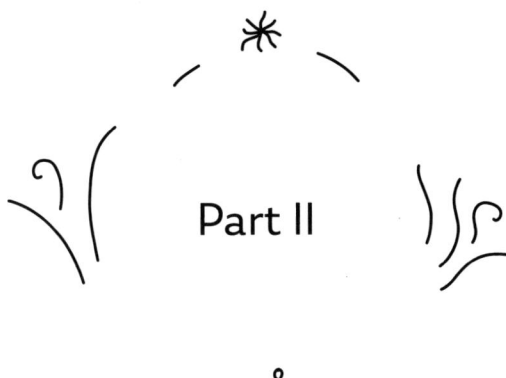

Chapter 14

The seventy-two-hour hold at Cedars-Sinai Hospital didn't cure anything, though it did give me a few days of rest from the world, a world now infected by the porn site. I went home, and a few days later returned to work. That was a stupid mistake. I should have asked for time off from the college, taken sick leave for at least a few weeks. Then again, being at home alone all those days could have ended badly. Michelle had to go to work at the high school, where she taught art. The kids would all be in school. Me wandering through the house by myself, with all sorts of tools at hand—knives, especially—was not a good idea. There was no one around to watch me. Perhaps that's why I decided to return to teaching so soon, to keep myself occupied.

Usually, teaching focuses me. I forget about everything else and pay attention to both the subject matter and the dynamics of the classroom. In one of the classes, we were studying *Light in August,* one of my favorite Faulkner books. It, like all of Faulkner's works, demands full attention. But I couldn't concentrate, couldn't come up with solid questions about the white man Joe Christmas and his "one drop" of African American blood in him. I stuttered through the classes. Afterwards I walked to the edge of the college property line and lit up. I've only smoked when I'm sick. The cigarettes calmed me, for as long as the smoke lasted. The nicotine somehow lifted my head slightly from all that was inside.

I was trying my best to forget the porn site, but that was impossible. The site had become an evil thing. It clung to me like rot. I longed for the year to pass, so as to try to buy my name back from the Russians. My computer science friend, who had traced the site back to St. Petersburg, said we could try to purchase it before the year was up. We tried. The pornographers were willing to sell it, for ten thousand dollars. Why? My name wasn't worth that much, and I certainly couldn't afford it. Perhaps they knew that anyone who was trying to buy their name back was desperate and would pay almost anything to retrieve it.

In the previous decade, I had published a book every other year. A couple collections of poetry, six novels, and a memoir. They hadn't been bestsellers in the least, but my name was making its way into a few corners of the literary world. I had written small essays that I performed for an NPR show called "Day to Day." I must have written over sixty essays for that gig. There was a new magazine in town, called "Tu Ciudad," which focused on Latinos in Los Angeles, and in which I had a monthly column. My work was getting out there. Then the porn site hit, which made me back away from the public like a crab pushing itself into its shell.

The mornings, when I write, are the most concentrated hours of the day—pure focus. But they became infected by not just the site, but what the site had drawn out of me. Through the years, I had learned certain psychological tricks through therapy—yes, I was a victim of incest rape; but I was more than that. My psychologist reminded me that, rather than succumbing to the trauma, I had built a life, and a good one. A strong marriage, loving children, a job, friends. And the writing—I had made it into the publishing world. He said that the relative would, through the years, make his appearance in my mind, as he had throughout my life. But there were ways to confront this, to stand back a bit and ask the questions with a forced objectivity: why is he back to haunt me now? What has set it off? That's why therapy was so important. It was a place where I could ponder these questions safely, to speak about them rather than let the trauma fester.

All that fell apart. Because of the website, the past haunted me. I couldn't step back and look at it with an objective eye. It just didn't stand before me, something to study and to deal with from arm's length. It was inside me; no—it *was* me. I was incest. That's all I could see.

The months passed. I got worse. I padded around the house, always wearing my pajamas. My appetite dwindled; I lost weight. The desire to drink came back—I had given it up a few years before, after getting on a medication that somehow turned off the need for alcohol—but Michelle didn't allow it, knowing that whiskey would do nothing but drop me deeper into the sinkhole of depression.

That antipsychotic I had been on, before the site, had done a good job of keeping me on a fairly even keel. I had been taking it for a few years and had enjoyed an equilibrium I hadn't felt all my life. Michelle had seen the changes. "You're calmer now. And you seem happier." It was true; I was happy. But the Internet had snapped through all that, had overcome the drug and left it to fall like dregs on the floor of my mind.

The psychiatrist prescribed more medication, another antipsychotic that I'd add to the first one. It didn't work. He put me on another drug. It had side effects; I twitched from it. So, he gave me yet another pill, which was supposed to deal with the twitching. It did, but I was still a wreck. The final drug he prescribed tipped me over the edge. My tongue started to flap around in my mouth, uncontrollably. I couldn't speak clearly in either language. Then the tongue stopped flopping and pushed itself back toward my throat. I thought I was going to swallow it.

He was the wrong psychiatrist for me. All those drugs, all at once; I felt poisoned from it. And they weren't working, they weren't curbing the horror that rose in me the moment I woke up. Nor was therapy, the place where I could leave my perturbed thoughts. My mind, my body, my very being, was soaked in the trauma.

It became too much. Months after the time at Cedars-Sinai, I started cutting myself again. The pain helped, for as long as it lasted. But I felt it coming on; I wanted, or felt compelled, to do more than cutting. That, and the shivers that plagued me, and the near-tongue-swallowing, pushed me to make a decision.

Michelle was at work. The kids were in school. I took my car keys and a small bag of clothes. In the car, something occurred to me. Something, for lack of better word, hopeful. Or protective. I went back into the house and grabbed a plastic resealable bag with a book in it, took it back to the car, placed it carefully in the clothes sack, and drove away. While on the 405, I called Michelle and told her I was checking in again. She asked me to repeat myself, she couldn't understand me with all the tongue spasms. I did. She said she would meet me there.

*

My second trip to the psych ward was very different from the first. I went to the ward at the UCLA Ronald Reagan Hospital, which was closer to home. They weren't as laissez-fare about treatment as was Cedars-Sinai. Medical students were all over, I could tell who they were by their young ages and slightly frantic look in some of their eyes. This psych ward was much busier than Cedars-Sinai, with all the students doing their clinicals. Nurses looked a bit flustered, having to deal with both us and the future psychologists.

At UCLA the doctors flushed me out. The withdrawal from all the meds was its own horror. My body turned against me. Uncontrollable shaking, vomiting, fuzzy sight, sweats—I felt like a stranger in my own body. In the rec room, they had me lie down on a sofa. Two nurses covered me with a blanket that must have weighed fifty pounds. My body still attacked me, but with the weights sewn into the fabric pressing down, I at least felt nested. I always had the plastic-bag-locked book in my hand, and I held it tight to my chest under the blanket. There I lay, for hours, while nurses tried their best to calm the loud and obstreperous, and shepherd the more-or-less stable to therapy sessions. I wanted to pull the weighted blanket over my head and smother.

After a couple of days, the shaking lessened, which meant I couldn't escape a group therapy session led by a student who didn't look older than sixteen. She was nervous. This might have been her first circle of the mentally ill. She talked about psychological things, and referred to papers on her lap, though she tried her best to keep eye contact with us before her sight darted back to the notes. We all stared at her, mute, while she suggested ways to mitigate our symptoms, such as finding distractions, something that, depending on my degree of sickness, has sometimes worked. Pick up a hobby. Exercise. Hang out with friends. Most of us looked defeated, as though we had tried all the tricks before, to no avail. One idea revealed how she was a little more naive about our diseases than you'd expect. Or maybe she was reading from the wrong notes, ones that sounded more suitable for a group of insane-lite. "One other thing you can do," she said, "is to think about someone who is suffering more than you are." She told us to give it some thought, about a minute's worth, then asked if anyone would like to share. No one volunteered. I was still twitching from withdrawal, and held the bagged book on my lap. The silence was too much for her. She asked a man sitting next to me, "How about you, Frank? Do you know someone who is suffering more than you?"

Frank looked like he was in his mid-twenties. He had thick, curly auburn hair, a deformed beard and a slash across the right side of his neck, about three inches long. Black crisscrosses of a good stitch job held the skin taut. He said, with no sarcasm, but as though he had truly considered the question, "I'm sorry, but no one comes to mind."

Looking back, I see the importance of having all those students around us. They were being trained in one of the best hospitals in the country. They were newbies, but they were kind, and they treated us with respect. The same young woman who held the group session later approached me in the rec room. I was sitting in a chair, the weighted blanket half covering me, and holding my book. "What's that?" she asked. I told her, just a book. She asked why I kept it in the bag. "It's falling apart," I said. She didn't ask any more about it, but turned to other subjects, such as springtime and the flowers that were blooming. She was a hiker. She'd explored nearly all the mountains surrounding Los Angeles. I told her my wife and I also hiked. We kept a nice conversation going. She wasn't nervous with me, as she'd been in the therapy circle. She asked about my family, the ages of my kids, my job, where I was from. I lied and said El Salvador. It seemed important to say that, to make myself all-Latino, rather than a bifurcated one.

At night, in bed, I clutched the book to my chest. I didn't take it out to read it, I just needed to have it with me at all times. It was a reminder of the good past, the days of searching for something I had lost in childhood.

At the end of the seventy-two-hour hold, they had me sit in a room with a dozen psychology students and one psychiatrist, who asked all the questions while her pupils took down notes on their laptops. Was I a threat to myself or to others? Did I feel like I could return to work? Would I stay on my meds? I asked her, which meds would I be on now? Because the hospital had done its job: they had begun the process of cleaning me out, stripping all the medication the psychiatrist had prescribed me. The rattles and shocks of withdrawal would stay with me for weeks after my release. But they planned to put me on a new, more refined regimen of pills.

They released me. I couldn't drive. Michelle picked me up. A friend came with her and drove my car home. We spoke little on the way back to the San Fernando Valley. Was she mad at me? Had I failed her once again? I apologized for it all. She wasn't angry; she was petrified. As were our children. I remember my daughter Raquel, who was in college, looking at my gauze-covered arms. It was too much for her. For a moment, she turned away, then turned back, rushed me and wrapped me in her arms. The rest of the family lined up and did the same. We did a group hug, with me in the middle, still clutching the bagged book and wailing.

I returned to work and writing. But the notion of starting another book exhausted me. The only place I could put pen to paper was in my journal. They are scrawls of entries; when I look back at them, I recognize that the madness was still in me, for months. I drew pictures—one was of a man strapped to the ground, tied to posts that stretched his limbs out straight. His mouth was a gaping *O*. It was too much to look at. I glued the pages together to cover him up.

One day I put on some Peter Gabriel songs and danced in a fury in my room. No one was home to witness it. It was as though I was trying to shake the horror out of me. It must have lasted a good half-hour; I kept playing the same songs over and again, then went into a whirling dervish of a dance, jumping up and down, trying to sing along with Peter while wearing myself out. I collapsed into the recliner. The calm lasted a few minutes. Then the tremors came over me again.

Nothing was working. My name, my *name*, had lost all its power; it had been raped by the porn site. Which means, I had been too. All the years of dealing with the past, looking at it straight-on, examining it in order to survive, crumbled.

After a few weeks, the meds started to sink in. They didn't take me out of the hole, but they helped me function. I could teach. I returned to writing poems. Instead of wearing pajamas all day, I forced myself to put on clothes. I could do all these things, but it was a struggle. Not just struggle—it was pain. I turned to the part of my life that I had cultivated through the years, and grabbed the thing that had, two decades previous, catapulted me into the journey of the self—the bagged book.

Chapter 15

The pages are yellowed. The spine is broken at least a dozen times. Years-old rubber bands hold the book together, crisscross. They've stayed stretched for too long, and have dried brittle. I should change them out. But they've become part of my art piece, this disintegrating copy of *Cien años de soledad*. In English, *One Hundred Years of Solitude*, by Gabriel García Márquez.

It's a paperback, the eleventh edition. I still keep it in the plastic bag, and I pull it out only after washing my hands. It's a pitiful thing and the most important book in my library. I've never shelved it. It's on a countertop in my office, always in sight. My talisman.

I can't read this copy anymore. It would crumble into dust. There are four other editions spread throughout the house, each in its own gradation of decay. Their spines are more or less intact. Each one, taken in succession, has fewer vocabulary translations written in the margins, unlike this first copy, which I ravaged with two ball point pens, red and black.

The last copy I recently bought in Colombia, a fiftieth anniversary, hardbound edition with artwork. I've yet to read it. I want to read it without a pen, without underlining lines of poignant moments in the story. I'd practically underlined every sentence in an earlier edition, when I had to rely less on a dictionary and was more freed-up to read it without so many vocabulary-seeking interruptions. With the special edition, I plan to keep all writing instruments out of arm's reach. It's too beautiful to mark up.

But it's not as beautiful as this first copy, this decrepit thing, this old man of a book that still whispers into my ear, in Spanish. It's not a book, really, but a parchment, an aged document that, since December of 1982, has unfolded before me. I have read *Cien años de soledad* every three or four years for over three decades. And it continues to unfold.

*

A few months after Michelle and I started dating, while we were still playing house in Father Bearden's home, my parents and I traveled to Mexico. An uncle in Mexico City had invited us to spend Christmas with his family. He even sent us money to cover the tickets. I didn't want to go. I was in love. A day without Michelle was pointless. I had planned to spend winter vacation in Iowa, rather than return to Tennessee. My mother was miffed. "You can't leave her for two weeks, to go to *Mexico*?" She shamed me into the trip.

We arrived on December tenth. On the twelfth, we, along with half of Mexico, visited the Catholic church in Tepeyac to see the cloth of Our Lady of Guadalupe. Thousands of people—mostly indigenous—walked on their knees to the church, where Juan Diego's four-hundred-year-old *tilma* (a type of serape) hung inside a glass cube. The story goes that Mary had presented herself to Juan Diego when he was a teenager. She was indigenous, or perhaps mestizo, a mix of Spain and Mexico. She spoke in Nahuatl, his native language. When he returned home, no one, not even the archbishop, believed him. Juan Diego trekked back to the site where he had met her and told her what happened. He made four trips back and forth between the hills and town. Finally, Mary told the boy to gather roses in his *tilma*. They were Castilian roses, which were not native to Mexico. When he returned to town, with the large bouquet in his arms, he dropped the roses at the archbishop's feet. The image of a pregnant Mary had penetrated the garment. The archbishop fell to his knees. He had the church built at the site in her honor.

I didn't understand. But I was moved to see thousands of people on their bloody knees, singing and praying rosaries. I didn't know what to think, but I was thinking. Fascinated, but there, in the church of Tepeyac that was flooded with pilgrims from all over the nation, I felt that strange and overwhelming cultural shame, worse than what I had felt in Father Murphy's apartment the night he had spoken Spanish to me.

And that uncle of mine didn't help. Tío Paco was a *pendejo*. At the time I didn't know that term. Some translate it as "asshole," which doesn't even begin to grasp the power of the Spanish word. According to my mother, a pendejo is a singular hair of the scrotum. Quite the insult. Everyone saw

Tío Paco as a charismatic man, full of life, a gentleman who liked his wine and danced with every woman in the room. But for me, in the beginning of the trip, Tío Paco was a pendejo.

In El Salvador, he had been a teenage guerrilla during a failed insurrection in 1932. The dictator, known as "El Brujo" (The Warlock) had ordered the massacre of more than twenty thousand indigenous men and women, all of whom were killed within two months. Tío Paco escaped. He fled to Mexico, where he later established a small bookstore. But his love for the Old Country never waned. Through the years he had made clandestine trips back to see family and old, surviving revolutionary friends.

Now, during our winter vacation, Tío Paco told us the histories of El Salvador, Mexico, Cuba, the United States, like an enthusiastic professor—no, *ecstatic*—something that appealed to me, although I didn't understand his lightning Spanish. Mamá had to translate for me.

Suddenly he turned to me and said, "Y ¿qué, vos sos guanaco pero no te conocés?"

Mamá translated: *You're Salvadoran but you don't even know who you are?* I turned mute. Shame and anger rose in me like bile.

I walked to the other side of the bookstore, trying to escape in the shelves. I was surrounded by books, all in Spanish, and I didn't recognize any title nor the authors, except one. Not his name, but the prize, *Nobel*. Gabriel García Márquez had won it that year. I pulled the book off the shelf and studied the cover. It was a surreal portrait, with nearly a dozen characters cluttered together. One man was reading a large parchment. Another sat at a table and fiddled with little fish made out of gold. An old, short, strong-backed woman scolded a giant man, and another young man was holding a baby that had a coiled pig's tail.

I read the title aloud. Tío Paco heard me. He looked at me, glanced at the copy of *Cien años de soledad* in my hand, and laughed. He said something between guffaws. It bothered Mamá, but she didn't say anything. I marched to her side and asked, "What did he say?" She didn't want to translate it. Uncle Paco was still laughing. "What did he *say*?"

She hesitated but finally answered, "Your uncle says you don't speak Spanish and you're going to read *that* book?"

That book, the one that I was about to reshelve. Now I clutched it like a grenade, shook it at my uncle's face and said to Mamá, "You tell *him* I'm going to *read* this book and someday I'll *understand* it!"

Mamá translated. Tío Paco quit laughing. He raised his eyebrows. His mouth formed an O, as though he recognized something in me, in my anger. Then he smiled. In that moment I saw something in his eyes. Hope? Pride? He turned to his cash register, took the book from me, and read the price. Mamá translated, "He says you owe him fifteen pesos."

I think Tío Paco saw a few drops of Salvadoran-ness in my tantrum. He quit harassing me. Now he hauled me from one corner of Mexico to another. The Templo Mayor, Teotihuacán, the Museum of Anthropology. He talked to me through my mother's translations. He spoke of the Aztecs, the Mayans, the Pipiles, and Nahuatl with authority and veneration. He was manic with the love of the Latin American world. He said "your people" while we stood before a Central American exhibit. *Your people. Your ancestry.* He had the energy of four professors in one, and sometimes spoke so quickly, Mamá couldn't keep up. She was exhausted, but she kept translating, as though recognizing the importance of the moment. I was worn out as well. So much Spanish. So many magnificent places, so much driving on dusty roads outside the city. Within the weariness, the root that my father had tried to rip out of my ground sprouted. A thin stem was breaking through.

One night, at Tío Paco's house, I went to bed and took a look at the novel. I translated the title in a whisper, "One Hundred Years of . . . *soledad*." I didn't recognize that last word. One hundred years of something. I opened the book and read aloud one of the most famous first lines in the history of global literature,

> Muchos años después, frente al pelotón de fusilamiento, el coronel Aureliano Buendía había de recordar aquella tarde remota en que su padre lo llevó a conocer el hielo.

Which is, in English,

> Many years later, as he faced the firing squad, Colonel Aureliano Buendía remembered back to that long-ago afternoon when his father took him to discover ice.

I recognized *muchos, años, frente,* and *hielo.* "Pelotón" sounded familiar . . . *pelo*? Ah, yes, *hair.* And "fusilamiento . . ." fuselage? Airplane, yes, of course. I wrote:

> Many years, in front of the airplane hair, Colonel Aureliano Buendía recorded a faraway tart inside his dad and they had some ice cream.

I was on a roll and kept going, guessing the words of the first ten lines, and wrote the translation in my journal. The next morning, I showed it to Tío Paco. He could read English. He read my translation, pressed his eyelids closed, and handed the journal back. He said, "Ay, púchica." He walked to a bookshelf, took out a Spanish-English dictionary, handed it over, and didn't charge me.

He wasn't as ebullient as he had been in the days before. At first, I thought it was exhaustion, after having spent a week teaching me about the Mexican and Central American worlds. It was more than that. He looked somber, lugubrious. He had circles under his eyes from lack of sleep. It was a drop, from the exuberant—manic—tour of the previous days, into a hole that was familiar. He smiled at me when he handed the dictionary over, but it was forced, as though he had lost all energy. I had seen this before, in my mother; I had seen it in me.

I was too enthralled by all those days of learning about our heritage to pay Tío Paco's mood swing much attention. He and Mexico had given me a focus. Now I longed to know my Salvadoran culture. We returned to the United States, back into a one-language world. There was no one to practice Spanish with.

But I had that book.

In Mexico, with the dictionary, I had translated the first three pages. Now, back in college, I pushed my homework to one side, placed the book on the desk, the dictionary beside it, and my journal at arm's reach. I recorded each word and its translation in columns of vocabulary, which I memorized, ten, twenty, then thirty words a day. They came rather easily. It felt as though I was slipping into the folds of my brain and reaching back to that four-year-old who grew up in Spanish-dominated San Francisco.

And my accent was similar to my mother's; again, I chalk this up to having heard it while living in the Mission District.

I read the pages of the novel aloud, with the new vocabulary in my head, and understood some of it, but not exactly. The scenes were so strange. The book began with a new world, where things had no name. It was like Genesis, but not really, as there was no god. I kept translating, memorizing, reading out loud to exercise my tongue. So many fascinating characters, such as Melquiades, a fat gypsy who sells artifacts to José Arcadio Buendía: two magnets, a telescope, and other everyday products of our world. In the world of the book, they were magical objects. Even a block of ice caused the characters to marvel. Yet other incidents, such as that of Remedios the Beauty, who is too beautiful for this world and who rises to the heavens with bed sheets as sails, were, for the characters, nothing to be amazed about.

I knew nothing of the novel's history, how, the moment it was published, it had spread across the Latin Americas like a California wildfire. It became *the* Latin American novel of the twentieth century. From there, it spread throughout the globe, in God knows how many translations. Its unique form captured the world's attention.

It didn't follow many of the rules of fiction. The naming of characters, for instance: a novelist should be careful to give them each a distinct name, so as not to confuse the reader. But in *Cien años*, names keep repeating themselves. There are no fewer than eighteen characters named Aureliano Buendía.

You have to stay on top of your game when reading the book, especially when the narrative leaps from one major event to another in the same sentence. Main characters die halfway through. The dead come alive. An insomnia epidemic wipes out everyone's memory. And incest is a real worry. The first time I came across the word, I knew what it meant without having to translate it. *Incesto*. That shook me. I wasn't sure if I could continue reading. But I did, still living in my manly, fuck-the-past phase. I wasn't going to let that one word get in the way.

It was like no other story I had ever read. Magic realism, the academics call it, a mix of the real with the otherworldly. It fascinated me, but something was missing: the community in which the novel was born. I was in the United States, living in a gringo, monolingual, magic-less world. The book couldn't become fully alive here, not for me, a young man whose need to return to his Latino roots now ached to the bone.

As did the need to write. The journals had changed. Now I wrote with a new purpose. The poetry turned to prose. Soon after meeting Michelle, I began writing a novel. This was sophomore year. It was a simple story about a young man in seminary who, due to circumstances I don't remember (I avoided the "Mead plot"), left dramatically. I finished it my junior year. It has never seen the light of day. It sits in a box somewhere in the shed out back. But that novel taught me a lot about writing, that it is a discipline, one that will take up most of your thoughts, all day long. My grades started to suffer and I didn't care, not with the manuscript thickening every day.

It also relieved the pressure in my brain. Waking up at five in the morning to write for three hours before an eight o'clock class made for better days. The writing cleared my mind, much like the running did. I shaped the semesters around the new desire, registered for afternoon classes, went to sleep earlier. It put more order to life and became a part of the regimen that kept my head on straight. I felt fewer mood swings.

The obsession has not left me. If too many days pass without writing, I grow antsy. Then the moods come on. I look back at that young man in those first days of writing that novel, and I see him happy. What had begun in high school with the journals, where I recorded both daily events and the questions of what was going on inside my skull, turned into a fledgling aesthetic. I was an English major, reading constantly. But the novels we read were more than just class assignments; they became mentors. I studied them not just as a student, but as a newborn writer who read with a pencil in hand, using it like a screwdriver to take the books apart and see what made them tick.

It was an effervescent time. I was in love with a woman who was on her own journey, her own commitment to peace and justice issues. For two years I had lived rent-free. The evening with Mead was behind me, as though it had never happened. And I was writing a barely concealed autobiographical novel, about a man who not only flees from seminary, but in the end, becomes an atheist. I still believed in God, but when I consider that first novel, I see that my notions of faith were beginning to crumble.

*

After we married, we moved to Iowa City, where I studied for a master's degree in English. There, we met activists, young and old, who were protesting Ronald Reagan's involvement in the covert wars in Central America. We worked with the Sanctuary Movement, which hid political refugees in churches to keep them safe from immigration authorities. We met people who had spent time in Nicaragua through an organization called Witness for Peace. They hosted groups that traveled the country for three weeks then returned to the United States to speak publicly about their findings. It was clear, through their reports, that too much was going on there, that our country was meddling in that nation's affairs. After talking with a number of people who had visited Central America, Michelle and I wondered if we could make the trip. But we had little money. I'm still not sure how we got through that time in Iowa City. Michelle had gotten a job at a health care facility that paid around $14,000 a year. Somehow, she not only put me through school, she covered the rent and food.

We had no plans after graduation. I, with a master's degree in English, was not exactly marketable. Michelle had studied sociology in college and planned to be a social worker. We didn't have any riches in mind; when it came to our future, we didn't have *anything* in mind. I had considered getting a PhD in literature, but my heart wasn't into it. All I wanted to do was write and become fluent in Spanish.

The illness was starting to emerge more, not so much the depression but the mania. The obsession over writing had grown. I wanted to spend more hours behind the typewriter. I slept little and wanted to sleep even less. Now I woke at four thirty every morning, made coffee and sat at the desk for hours, working away at another novel, before having to rush out of the apartment and make my first class. The desire to search out my Latino roots also took up a lot of space in my mind. I took Spanish classes and read *Cien años de soledad* at night.

It was much like junior year in high school: I could do so much and not tire. But the anger was brewing more. It was all about Central America. It made no sense, I yelled, to be studying literature while Nicaraguans were murdered by US-backed terrorists and death squads were shaking

El Salvador to its knees. It was more than that, of course, but I gave no thought to the source of the rage. The simmering fury wasn't about childhood abuse, or homophobic teenagers, or predator priests. It had its roots in the suffering of others. I would tell myself this for a decade.

We couldn't visit Nicaragua, not on Michelle's salary. But we both wanted to. Before meeting me, Michelle had considered working overseas. Once married, she figured that dream would end. A three-week trip to another country to learn firsthand what was going on, and reporting on those goings-on upon returning to the States, could be the next best thing. But how? I said, "Hell, let's just move to Nicaragua!"

"How can we do that? We can't afford it."

"We can join the group that works there, Witness for Peace."

Michelle's heart is a bit cleaner than most. She wanted to go overseas to help the poor. I did too, but I had my own agenda. Nicaragua wasn't El Salvador, but they were neighbors. That was the idea—get back to my roots. Live at the source, or as closely as I could. I wanted to get the hell out of the United States and fight for Central American liberation. I didn't know that my ideals were in part fueled by the abuse and sickness. But in recollection I see that they, as much as the Liberation Theology classes, had catapulted me into the anger. Now I had a focal point where to put it. Not the past, but Reagan. The war in Nicaragua. The Salvadoran death squads.

But the anger wasn't always focused. I was trying to keep it together, to believe that my hotheadedness was simply a sign of my romantic, manly, live-life-to-the-fullest Latino heritage. In our first year of marriage, Michelle again witnessed what was to become part of her future. The sudden bursts of emotion, the borderless euphoria, the plummet into depression during the shortened days of winter. And the anger, one that could be uncontrollable in one moment and as honed as a razor in the next. Stress set me off: a telephone bill, a busted carburetor, essays to write for class. The nights of insomnia worked against me.

One morning, after two days of little sleep, I sat at the table, slumped over, with the manual typewriter before me, blank paper to the left, the growing manuscript to the right. I didn't move. Michelle knew, the moment she saw me, that something was wrong. She had to get to work, but must have been afraid to leave me alone. She leaned over and put her hand on my shoulder. She asked if I was all right. I spilled out all that was in my head, mostly about the inability to write. She was about to say something else, something of comfort, when I punched the typewriter's base with my palms. The machine flew off the desk and crashed against the floor, leaving a large nick in the linoleum.

Michelle jumped when the typewriter hit the floor. But that was it. She scolded me. Her face turned as hard as marble. She raised her hand like a cop at a crossroad, and said, "I'm not putting up with this shit," then walked out and slammed the door. The scold was enough, that Iowan, German honesty that won't put up with fools. Somehow, I hadn't broken the typewriter. I placed it back on the table and began writing.

The more we got involved in community organizing in Iowa City, the more the idea of going to Nicaragua solidified. We attended lectures from people who had visited there. They had mentioned the Witness for Peace "Long Termers," the people who were their hosts while in Nicaragua, North Americans who spent months, and even years, in the war zones. They were paid paupers' salaries, but their expenses were covered—plane flight, room and board. If we applied to be Long Termers, we could afford to go. We filled out the paperwork. I graduated. Witness for Peace accepted us. Three months later we moved to Nicaragua.

Chapter 16

Michelle and I sat on the curb of a dirt road in the small village of El Jícaro, Nicaragua, waiting for cows to explode. She was drawing in her journal. I was reading *Cien años de soledad* again, but kept both my dictionary and grammar book in my backpack. I didn't want to balance all three books on my lap at the same time, like a student cramming for an exam, not with a dozen Nicaraguans sitting on the same curb, waiting for a ride, waiting to see if cow guts and bone would fall from the sky. They made jokes about it. One woman put out her arms and said that if she was lucky, she'd catch an entire loin. But there were grumbles. The Sandinista soldiers who moseyed the cows down the road heard our gripes, but said nothing. They moved the herd before them and took the main road out of town. If any cow stepped on a land mine, the Sandinistas would pay the poor farmer from whom they'd borrowed the cattle.

No vehicle could leave the town until after the soldiers returned—hopefully with the entire herd intact—and pronounced the road safe to travel. It had gotten bad. The enemy, known as the Contras, planted land mines outside of towns to knock out Sandinista army personnel carriers. But this put the civilian population at risk. It surprised no one; the Contra forces were known to attack civilians as well as soldiers. That was how they had been trained.

The cows were a comfort. They were also a rarity—what farmer was ready to give up his herd to a road of land mines, no matter how much the Sandinistas paid him? And it wasn't uncommon for a poor, uneducated, humble farmer to argue with a Sandinista officer and refuse to hand over his cattle. These were new days, days of no dictatorships nor bloody military forces that attacked their own people. The woman who had pretended to catch meat that rained from the sky started to lose her patience. She approached the captain. "When in God's name are we going to leave? I've got to get to Ocotal before the market closes." She motioned to the bags of mangos next to her. "They'll rot by the time we get there." She sounded like a mother reprimanding her son. The captain listened and promised her it would be soon.

It wasn't soon. It never was. Sometimes, when no cows were on hand, we had to wait for a platoon of soldiers to walk the roads, their AK-47s at the ready, their heads down, and their eyes peeled open, searching for the buttons of buried mines.

For months before leaving the States, Michelle had become as diligent as I in studying Spanish. She memorized vocabulary and worked through a grammar book. We talked with the refugees in the Iowa City Sanctuary every chance we could. They became our patient tutors.

In Nicaragua, we spoke only Spanish. It was our group's rule, a way to blend in as much as two gringos in a third world country can blend. To speak in English just made for another border between us and the Nicaraguans. If we spoke in Spanish—as crackly as our Spanish was—people might be more comfortable to talk with us, to allow us into their conversations. And getting into conversations with Nicaraguans was part of our job description: to interview people who had suffered under the hands of the Contras.

No cows exploded that day. We, along with the crowd of travelers, climbed aboard pickups and cattle trucks. According to the Sandinista captain, the roads were safe. But for the first few miles, the driver of the cattle truck we rode in drove slowly and studied every small rock on the road to make sure it wasn't the top of a buried bomb. I looked over the side of the railings and stared at the thousand hoof prints that the cows had left behind.

We had been in-country for about two months. Our plan that day was to spend a couple of nights in Ocotal, the capital of the state of Nueva Segovia, which was butted up against the Honduran border. Ocotal was still in the war zone, but it was a much larger town, with more Sandinista soldiers protecting it from the Contras. After spending weeks traveling from one village to another, a few days in Ocotal would be akin to a spa resort. It had paved streets in the center of town, but the rest were dirt and, in the rainy season, six-inch-deep mud. All the buildings were adobe and looked like they'd been built over a hundred years ago, during horse carriage days. Ocotal offered more hostels to choose from, though none of them with five-star ratings. But as long as there was a bed, a hose for bathing, and a common latrine, we were happy.

*

In 1985, Nicaragua was in a revolution. The people had overthrown a dictator named Anastasio Somoza six years previous. They had their own guerrilla force—the Sandinistas—but it had been a popular uprising. People had taken to the streets in protest, even with Somoza's National Guard soldiers encircling them.

Somoza was a terrorist. He had spent decades in the presidential palace and had slaughtered his own people all those years, all in the name of anticommunism. One of his favorite tactics was having dissidents pushed out of high-flying airplanes into the Pacific Ocean. His death squads, created by the National Guard soldiers who dressed as civilians at night, were ubiquitous, both in the cities and the countryside. They pulled people out of their homes and cut them to pieces with machetes. They left the bodies on the roadsides or in town plazas as a warning to everyone to stay away from any suspected communists.

It took nearly twenty years of guerrilla warfare and national protests, but in 1979, thousands of Nicaraguans and Sandinista soldiers gathered in Managua's main plaza, while Somoza fled to Miami. The Sandinistas became the government. It didn't take long for them to get to work revolutionizing the country: free health care for all, a literacy campaign that reached most every village in the nation, and the redistribution of hundreds of thousands of acres of land to poor farmers, land that had been in the hands of the elite for decades. It was a nationally effervescent time, with an excitement that was still in the air six years later, when we arrived.

But the excitement had been tempered by war. It was an indirect war with the United States. Ronald Reagan, who had been railing against communist influence in Central America since my years in seminary, created the Contras out of the same National Guard forces that had once protected Somoza.

Witness for Peace had been founded three years previous, when a group of North Americans learned about a child's head being cut off by a US military mortar in the town of Jalapa, near the border with Honduras. They went to investigate. They weren't the only foreigners in the country; people from all over the world visited Nicaragua to experience the revolution. But Witness for Peace had a specific mission: to stand with the Nicaraguan people, which meant leaving the safety of Nicaragua's capital, Managua, and entering the war zones. They noticed that wherever a group of gringos traveled, Reagan's Contras would not attack. How could they? What would happen if Dan Rather reported on a group of American citizens killed by a US-backed military force? It would be terrible publicity. Reagan might be forced to pull his troops out. In our own way, we could help end the war.

These were lofty, idealistic notions, and I make no apologies for them. I don't know how much effect we had on saving people's lives. Even then, some among us struggled with the work itself—was ours not just another form of self-righteous US intervention, though it was for a good cause? But most Nicaraguans we met seemed happy to know us, as though opening a curtain to say, *See what our revolution has done? See the changes we have made?*

We had landed at the Augusto Cesar Sandino International Airport, which had suffered during the war. Shells of duty-free boutique stores were lined up and down the hallways, empty of their wares. Windows were blown out. There was no air conditioning. The humid Nicaraguan air lay over our skin the moment we'd stepped out of the plane. Sandinista soldiers walked the corridors. There were posters of Cesar Sandino, the Stetson-wearing revolutionary from the 1920s and the inspiration of the new government's name—*Sandinista*.

A fellow named Jaime, a Nicaraguan who worked for Witness for Peace, picked us up in a dead-gray Toyota Corolla that might have dated back to the original year of production. Michelle and I had to push it while Jaime held it in neutral. He kicked it into first, over and again, until the motor finally turned over. We jumped in. It didn't have a muffler. Nor did it have a floor in the front passenger seat, just a rotted-out hole. There was also a small hole under Jaime's shoes. I thought about the Flintstones, going on a drive, using our feet for propulsion.

Jaime was Nicaraguan, but had lived several years in the States, where he had studied history at Stanford. His was a clipped, precise English. He had planned to get his PhD and teach somewhere in the United States, but the revolution had beckoned him home. "There is nowhere else I would rather be," he said, and he talked about the radical changes that the country had gone through since the end of the dictatorship.

He took us to a house in Managua, where a few of the Long Termers lived. Most of them wore ragged T-shirts and old, faded jeans. They were all gringos like ourselves. Most of them were somewhere between their mid-twenties and early thirties. They looked worn out.

Michelle and I weren't the only new Long Termers. We were a group of nine new recruits who, before going into the war zones, would have to be trained on *how* to live in those zones. What stupid mistakes to avoid. How to gain the people's trust so they would tell us about their experiences living in a war. They told us that we would spend a lot of time hitchhiking. They taught us how to stand alongside the Nicaraguan people. Sometimes it meant just hanging out in a town that was under threat. We had to get involved with local events, such as religious celebrations and national holidays. It also meant gathering stories from people who had survived Contra attacks. We would write up those reports and send them to the offices of congresswomen and men in Washington, DC, to persuade them to vote against Reagan's funding of the Contras.

We, along with our new colleagues, were itchy to get out there and start standing with the people. We were raring and ready to get to work, but one of the goals of the Long Term trainers was to knock the shit out of our idealistic notions before we stepped foot outside of Managua. It was only a two-week training course, but in that time, they packed us with everything from the history of Nicaragua to how to boil water before drinking it.

We weren't all gringos. The team also had local Nicaraguan organizers who sat with us during our sessions and spoke Spanish that sounded much like my mother's. They weren't ones to back down or to cower before foreigners. I remember a man named Ricardo who said that, though he was happy that we were there to join them in their struggle, he didn't want us to become "problematic." We weren't sure what he meant, so he laid it out: Latin America had suffered under the hands of outsiders for five hundred years, even do-gooders, such as missionaries. We were gringos; it was in our blood to get involved in other countries' politics. And though we had come to help Nicaragua in its time of need, he said, we didn't know a damn thing about what it meant to live here.

Some of us took umbrage with that. They didn't care for being reprimanded. I liked it, for some reason. I'm not sure why, except that I was young, looking for my roots, and getting more manic as the days passed. So much had changed: Michelle and I had catapulted ourselves from the small activism in Iowa City into an international struggle. It was true life. It was *sexy*.

A woman named Elizabeth, who was the office manager of Witness for Peace, walked out onto the large front porch where we were meeting. She said that it was time to give us a break, and why not take us all out for lunch? We, gringos and Nicas both, piled into a small bus with large windows. Ricardo took the wheel.

We drove through Managua, which was a rubble heap of a city, having been leveled by an earthquake thirteen years before. After a couple of miles, Ricardo took a left and drove over a one-lane dirt road that led into a forest on the edge of the city. He drove a long while. When we had first boarded the bus, our spirits had lifted, though some still grumbled over Ricardo's words about invading gringos. Now, after half an hour of driving through the woods, we got quiet. "Where's the restaurant?" one of us asked.

"It's in a village on the other side of the woods," Ricardo said, "about another half hour. It's worth it, they make the best tamales."

Twenty minutes later, nearly a dozen men walked out from behind trees. They had masks on, kerchiefs around their faces, with only their eyes showing. Some wore old, faded baseball caps. They looked ragged, as though having spent their lives in the woods. They were armed. Two of them stood on the small road and raised their rifles to stop the bus. They acted quickly. One banged on the door. Ricardo froze. The soldier banged again and cursed. Ricardo opened the door. "¡Fuera! ¡Fuera!" the soldier yelled (Get out! Out!). He held the rifle in both hands. It wasn't an AK-47, the official armament of the Sandinistas. It looked more like a rifle my father would use on a hunt.

We scrambled off the bus. The other armed men surrounded us. The one in charge told them to separate us into two groups. They grabbed our arms and pulled us away from one another. The leader said to take the gringos over to one side of the woods and the traitorous Nicaraguans to another, "behind those trees." Michelle and I stood next to each other, holding hands. One soldier grabbed her arm and pulled her away from me. "Todo bien, todo bien," he said softly, reassuring her all would be okay. He turned to another soldier, then pointed at me, "Jale este hijo de puta allá con los demás de los traidores." (*Take this son of a bitch over there with the rest of the traitors.*) The soldier obeyed: he raised a pistol, snatched my arm, and hauled me away from Michelle.

I looked back at her. The Contra soldier was still pulling her away, putting her with the rest of the new Long Term recruits, whom he tried to pacify, saying in broken English, "It will be all right. We will get you home." The soldier who had grabbed me pushed me into the woods. I stumbled into the small group of Nicaraguans behind the tree line. Ricardo was there, his hands up, his eyes to the ground. I couldn't see Michelle, though I heard her: she called out my name. Right then the soldier raised his pistol, put the muzzle six inches from my forehead and pulled the trigger. It clicked. He said, in clear, precise English, "Bang. You're dead."

The simulation was over. The one who had shot me pulled off his kerchief. It was Jaime, the man who had picked us up at the airport. His face was covered with camouflage paint. He smiled and patted my back. I shook.

They gathered us all together and told us what a lousy job we had done. Ricardo said, "What did we tell you at the house? Stay together! Grab hold of each other and don't let go, don't let the Contras separate you. If they do, they'll leave you all," pointing to the white Long Termers, "somewhere on the edge of a town, and tell you to get out of the country. Then they'll take *them*," he pointed at the Nicaraguans, and let loose with everything that would happen to us: Guttings. Getting hanged. Shot.

I don't know how much of it our group was soaking in. Everyone trembled. Some cursed. We boarded the bus. They took us to a *comedor*, where we ate tamales and drank lots of beer. Revolutionary songs played on a boom box. Some of us were loosening up. Others groused about Ricardo, who had scolded us so. Michelle was having a hard time eating her *tamal*. For we had made ourselves a promise before leaving the States: no matter what happened, we wouldn't separate from each other.

She excused herself from the table and walked outside. I followed her. She wept and trembled and wondered if we had made a mistake. I held her tightly and said it was just a simulation, that nothing like that would happen to us, as though I believed it, as though I wanted nothing to happen.

I shook, not with fear, but excitement. And a little confusion. I looked nothing like a Nicaraguan. I asked Ricardo about this. "You could pass for a city-boy. One of our lighter-skinned people, someone from the upper class." He talked more about class, something the country had to confront to make all people equal, but I heard about half of it. For the "Contras" had seen me as a Nicaraguan. They had separated me from my fellow gringos. They had put a fake gun to my head. They had recognized me for what I was, and what I wanted to become even more: A Latino. I was ecstatic.

Chapter 17

I had begun to fiddle with my name decades before learning that some who have survived childhood sexual abuse do the same. I can trace it back to sophomore year in high school. It was in class, I don't know what the subject was, but I was bored and writing in my notebook while the teacher droned on. For some reason, I started playing with my first name. Actually, in recollection, it feels more like discovery than fiddling. I made one change: I cut the "k" and replaced it with "c"—*Marc*. The name sounded the same, but its appearance on the page had completely changed, had morphed into something mysterious and clean. I played with it for a while, even wrote it on class assignments, until a teacher said, "You've forgotten how to spell your *name*?"

I went back to using the "k" and thought little more of it, until the day my English teacher, old Mrs. Blandon, smiled at me and, out of the blue, said, "Marcus Aurelius, how are you today?" She was one to give us elevated nicknames, and she called me that for the rest of the semester. At times she addressed me by my new last name; I became Mr. Aurelius. It thrilled me.

It was a short-lived nickname. No one picked up on it. There were official papers to fill out: driver's license, transcripts, diploma. I had to use my birth-given name. It's obvious what it was. But I can't stand to pronounce it, or think upon it. And to put it on paper is an act of pure violence against myself. I won't write it down. I can't, not if I want to continue to survive childhood. I haven't written it since our first days in Nicaragua, when we had to fill out forms.

In Managua, we had to get an ID card as well as some travel papers that allowed us entry into the war zones. I filled in the slots. The application had blank spaces for both my parents' surnames. I didn't understand this.

Why would they need to know my mother's last name, since she had taken my father's? The lady at the desk looked at me as though I should have understood, and said, simply, "because that's your name. Your full name."

Epiphany.

According to the nation of Nicaragua, I had two last names. Everyone did, even though some might introduce themselves with only one. But on paper at least, you honored both sides of the family. I was about to write my first name, but hesitated. I remembered, suddenly, those high school days when I had first started to tool around with it. But now, the fiddling had purpose. I decided to lie, just a little. I took the original name, lopped off the "k," and added "cos." *Marcos*. Now, somewhere in the shed beside our house, in an old box of memories, there's an ID card with what is now my official name: Marcos McPeek Villatoro. Official, because after leaving Central America, I applied for the name change through Sacramento. Now, my birth certificate, along with my driver's license, passport, and checkbook, has my full-out name.

I don't know how many incest survivors do this, though I have met a few who have changed their names completely. Jim Brown becomes Herman McBride. Sarah Long finds comfort in Mary Lyons. It's a form of stripping out the old, original name, which is pockmarked with the violence. Do everything you can to separate yourself from the horror.

I didn't need to tear up my old name, but rather I used the rules of Latin America to reshape it. It is now over forty years old, and it has helped. The thought of my original name makes me shudder. Whenever someone from the distant past uses it, I want to smash something. Calling me by the monosyllabic name with the "k" at its end feels like brutality.

When I changed my birth certificate, I obligingly kept the McPeek in, following the Latin American cultural norms. But it was more than that: I didn't want to hurt my father's feelings, no matter what had happened in the past.

I have Nicaraguan bureaucracy to thank for this. At the time, I had no idea that filling out those papers was helping me survive childhood. All I knew was that Nicaragua, within the first few days of us being there, was pulling me closer to my Central American roots. It renamed me. It gave me back a part of myself.

We who have been trapped in the evil acts of others must grab hold of every choice we can. Victims must take control of their lives to survive. We redefine ourselves, so that we are more than just the outcome of others' sins. For some of us, to change one's name is more than just a radical act. It is a revolution of the mind. It took Nicaragua's revolution to teach me this. Another reason I love that country so.

Witness for Peace assigned Michelle and me to the state of Nueva Segovia, in the north of the country, right against the Honduran border. We hitchhiked from Managua to Ocotal, more than a hundred miles of jumping from one pickup truck bed to another, depending on how far the driver was going. We rarely took buses, as they were always chock full, with some passengers sitting on the tied-down luggage on the roof. We left Managua at eight in the morning. By the time we arrived in Ocotal, it was night. That didn't help Michelle's nerves. The simulated Contra attack was still working on her. Hitchhiking on country roads in the mountains after sundown was dangerous. You never knew if the Contras would decide to attack after dark.

The simulation was also working on me, but not in the same way. It was a prelude for what was to come: Finally, we were getting out into the war zone! Not only was I looking for my Latin American roots; I was also seeking out action. Wasn't that why we came here? To witness, firsthand, what it meant for a country to be at war? To stand among a people who were suffering our country's foreign policy? I wasn't scared, but *excited*. As the sun set, before we reached Ocotal, I scanned the woods and hills for the enemy. Would they surround us as our colleagues had in Managua? Or would they just start shooting? Or would they see Michelle's blond hair—the only blond in the open truck—and pull back, knowing that there was a gringa on board? Because our mentors had said it back on the porch in Managua: That hair, and her white skin, could keep an attack at bay.

In Ocotal, we found a hostel that made the house in Managua feel like a luxury condo. Someone had smeared what looked like dried shit on the walls. The stained mattress had no bed sheets or blankets. Gray spiders the size of your hand crawled the walls, or just clung, unmoved, to the adobe. I took a newspaper to them. They left grease marks on the wall.

Later, after living several months in Nicaragua, that same hostel would become our oasis from the hardships in the countryside. A hardship that we, as gringos, could leave at any time. But we were Long Termers on an eight-month contract. Already, I was making plans never to return to the United States.

Ocotal was not our base of operations. We would spend most of our time in the countryside, traveling from one village to another, organizing trips for US citizens who came to Nicaragua on the three-week fact-finding tours. Part of our job was to take busloads of fellow foreigners through our section of the war zone, for them to meet local people and see, firsthand, how the war was affecting the country. The delegates would return to the States and speak to their communities about what they had learned. Michelle and I had to set up meetings with local organizations, such as the Mothers of the Disappeared, women who had lost their children to Contra kidnappings and murder.

Michelle was a natural for the job. She was an organizer to the bone, and knew how to pay attention to details when putting together a tour. She and I met with the local groups to set up dates of arrival. She was very enthused. For her, the greatest goal was to get the word out, back to the States, to stop Reagan from destroying Nicaragua.

I *hated* delegation work. It was everything I was against—I didn't come to Nicaragua to hang out with gringos all the time. I was there to be a witness to the war. I came to stick myself as deeply as possible into the culture, without the hindrance of a bunch of US citizens roaming through the countryside. Michelle and I argued about this. "You know the job," she said. "We're here to host the delegations." I said that no, we were here to keep the Contras at bay, with our mere presence. We were to travel to villages and listen to the people who had suffered atrocities under the hands of the Contras.

I didn't mind setting up the schedules with Michelle, for that meant making acquaintances, and some friendships, with people in small mountain villages such as Jalapa, Jícaro, and San Juan del Rio Coco. My Spanish was taking on a Nicaraguan lilt. I could feel it; I was approaching my mother's world. It was when we brought in the busload of delegates that I cringed. They looked like a gaggle of tourists emptying out of the bus to spend a day at Disneyland, with large floppy hats, sunglasses, thick sunscreen, cameras hanging off their necks, and the loud English that ricocheted off the plaza walls.

I think the exhaustion, that of a North American roaming around in a third world, war-torn country, kept the mania from taking over during our first months there. I was hungry for my roots, but I also craved peanut butter more than a human being ought. I longed for good whiskey, a comfortable bed, daily warm-water showers. The longer we were in the country, the less these cravings ate at me, until someone from a delegation would pull out a small jar of Skippy. I'd eat more than half of it, with a spoon and no bread. It was another reason for me to hate the delegations: they brought those delights to us. They kept us tied, through food and drink, to the United States. My own country, from which I wanted a divorce. New forms of hatred and love rose in me: loathing for the nation I was born in, and pure cariño for the country that was, slowly, making its way under my skin. It wasn't El Salvador, but I had plans. After our work in Nicaragua, I would make sure we moved to my mother's home country, where we would live the rest of our days.

My mind sparked with self-promises. The conviction to remain in Central America grew with the passing weeks. I was getting agitated; I wanted to see the war, wanted to see battles raging on the outskirts of a village. The mortars that went off in the distant mountains, I wanted to see up close. I wanted to squat alongside the soldier who shot it. Everyone we spoke with, I gathered their vocabulary, words that I had not heard before (*matanza*—massacre; *degollado*—cut throat; *pertrechos*—ammunition), and wrote them in my journal.

Spanish became everything. At night I studied the grammar book as if preparing for exams. After a while, I could run through the conjugations in a snap: To eat, for example: Yo como/tú comes/él come/nosotros comemos/ellos comen. Past tense, present tense, future, conditional, I could do them all.

Then there was the subjunctive, the conjugation that throws off many an English-only speaker, even more than the use of the masculine-feminine, which gives every object a sexual orientation. The subjunctive takes the speaker into the unknown. In English, we say, "When I eat lunch with John, I'll tell him about my new car." *When I eat lunch* has a sense of assurance: I *will* eat lunch with John. That's not how it works in Spanish: you twist the verb "comer" into another word. It's not "Yo como" anymore, but "Yo coma." You don't say "Cuando como con John," but "Cuando coma con John," which denotes a sense of unsurety: "When I eat with John—that is, if I don't get in a car wreck, or I can't find the restaurant, or there's not an earthquake, or if someone doesn't drop a vase of flowers on my head from a second-story window—I'll order pupusas." It's as though, in Spanish, within the very structure of the language, you recognize that nothing is assured, that anything can happen on the way to lunch. English has all but lost the subjunctive tense. In Spanish, it shows up in every other sentence.

I learned the subjunctive as though my life depended on it. But in Nicaragua, the grammar book could only take me so far. There were other words here that took a while to catch on to. Take another aspect of Central American Spanish that's a little hard for the monolingual English speaker to understand: there are two forms of the second-person singular pronoun "you:" *Usted* and *tú*. "Usted" is a "formal" address, used when you first meet someone, or you're talking with your mother or anyone older than you. "Tú" is more familiar, used among friends, or a mother speaking to her child. The very relationship is rooted in these words.

But in Central America, there's one "you" that you won't find in a grammar book: *vos*. It is the most intimate of the three. And it changes the conjugation: instead of saying *Usted habla* (you talk) or *tú hablas*, in Central America you've got the third choice. With *vos*, the accent is on the final syllable: *Vos hablás*. It's hard to translate exactly into English, but I interpret it as "We're so close, I would die for you." That may seem over the top, but for me, it evokes the meaning and power of the word.

They used *vos* a lot in Nicaragua. People who first met us and learned about our work, and saw us as fans of their revolution, would skip over *Usted* and *tú* to "vosear" with us in the first few minutes of a conversation.

This unique form of "you" fascinated me. To go beyond the intimacy of *tú* meant digging even deeper into my heritage. I used *vos* a lot, maybe too much. Later, back in the States, while visiting my abuelita Romilia, I made the mistake of using it on her. She was sick with the beginning stages of

Alzheimer's and was losing much of her memory. But the moment I said *vos* to her, her head cleared up. She rose from her bed, looked at my mother and pointed at me. "¿Quién es este malcriado que se atreve a decirme vos?" ("Who is this spoiled brat who dares to call me vos?"). I learned then to be more sparing with the word, to use it only with the most intimate of friends.

*

Magdalena García Montenegro lived in a ramshackle adobe house on a hill that overlooked the town of Jícaro, a village that became our headquarters. It was smack in the middle of the war zone, though it hadn't experienced any attacks or battles in some time. It was tucked in a valley, surrounded by hillocks on all sides. The plaza was small, with the government building on one side and the Catholic church on the other. Quiet; as quiet as Rogersville, in Tennessee. During the day there were few men in town, as most went out to work the corn crops.

Magdalena was a stout woman in her early forties whose low, guttural voice could match Lauren Bacall's. She had kind eyes that could also slice whenever someone groused about the Sandinistas. She was a widow. Her husband had been murdered during the Somoza days. She had three children, two daughters and one son. He had joined the Sandinista army and now was with an outfit in the state of Matagalpa. The girls still lived at home.

It was yet another shack of a house, like most homes in the area, with two bedrooms, one which Magdalena used as a chicken coop (and where we slept). The kitchen, which was no more than an adobe stove, stood outside, under a laminated canopy. They had a small living room, which was filled with knickknacks: family pictures of her son, her daughters and deceased husband, a crucifix nailed into the adobe wall, a small framed portrait of Our Lady of Guadalupe, and a huge poster of Sandinista soldiers storming into battle.

Magdalena made the best coffee on the planet. She owned a few coffee trees. She picked it during harvest time, laid out an old tarp on her dirt yard, and spread the fruit over it evenly so the sun could dry the ruddy skin and pulp off the bean. After a couple of days of blistering sun, Magdalena cleaned the rotting pulp off the tarp to let the beans dry. Afterwards she roasted them in a cast iron skillet, just enough to last a few days, to make the coffee stretch between harvests. The smell of coffee in a skillet, there's nothing like it. She had her own grinder. Once the coffee had cooled in the pan, she filled the wooden grinder with beans and twisted the handle dexterously, aggressively, until the final crack of bean split under the metal corkscrew. She made everyone else's coffee in a large pot, in which she poured milk and sugar, to cook them all together. For me, she had a small aluminum pot that she filled with pure, black coffee, no sugar, no milk, which, for Nicaraguans, was a strange, very gringo thing. She poured the sweet coffee for Michelle and her daughters, then poured mine, shaking her head as she did, "Bitter coffee for such a sweet man," she'd say.

The longer we lived in Nicaragua, the more comfort we found in the little things, such as stability. Michelle and I were on the road constantly, hitchhiking from one village to another to follow up on Contra reports, and to set up meetings for the delegations. We spent more time in Jícaro than other towns, in part to plan for the tours and in large part to rest. Magdalena's home became our countryside oasis. That coffee of hers was enough to keep me coming back.

I liked staying with Magdalena because hers was the fastest, most fluid, most difficult Spanish to keep up with. It challenged Michelle's and my ears; if you could understand Magdalena, you could understand anybody. We would sit for hours and talk about any subject that came to mind. Michelle showed pictures of her family. Magdalena stared and said, "So, they're all blonde, like you? How beautiful!"

It was porch chat, but Magdalena held court. We'd listen to her stories, from her childhood all the way to her dead husband, her son who was at war, the corn and coffee harvests, and the Contras—she growled that word—who didn't have the guts to take the Sandinistas head-on, so they turned against the civilians. In our first visits, Michelle and I had a hard time keeping up. But as time passed, Magdalena's proclamations became clearer and clearer. She fed my need never to return to the States. She roused something in me—the excitement; the simmering euphoria; the rage against my own country. But she didn't just affect me like that. Michelle got caught up in her stories as well. She was becoming as fluent as I, even her Midwest accent was starting to take a Nicaraguan turn. She wasn't afraid anymore. The simulation back in Managua was behind us. We had traveled the northern part of the country with no mishaps, no Contra attacks. Sometimes we heard the gunfire from a battle raging on the other side of a ridge, but we became as accustomed to it as the local Nicaraguans, who measured the danger by the distance of the sound.

At night, in Magdalena's home, I studied my grammar book and lists of vocabulary words and read a few pages of *Cien años de soledad*. I also wrote in a journal, in clunky Spanish, about our experiences. Magdalena seemed to understand my need for some solitude, even if it were just half an hour. She would leave me alone and hush the children, "Quiet. Don Marcos is working."

Don. It was a reminder of who we were, and how the Nicaraguans saw us. I didn't deserve the title; I was just twenty-three, a good two decades younger than Magdalena. But she, like others, addressed me with the word used for older men, or men who had power. She used *usted* with us. It reminded me that we *did* have power. We were from the United States. Even Magdalena, who suffered no fools, fell to addressing me like that, until I asked her not to. "I don't deserve that," I said. She didn't balk. "All right then, Marcos. I'll address you like I do my son. Which means I can scold you too." She laughed. From then on, whenever she said "you" to me, she used the intimacy of *vos*.

*

Magdalena introduced us to the small group of women who called themselves The Mothers of the Disappeared. Each had lost a child—usually a son—to the Contras. They lived in villages surrounding Jícaro and made the trek into town to meet with us. About a dozen women arrived. We gathered in the Catholic church, sitting on old, splintery pews that we had arranged in a triangle.

At first, you wouldn't have known this was a group of women who mourned for the loss of their children. They talked with one another and laughed and traded gossip. They spoke with us politely, asked where we were from, had either of us been to Los Angeles, California? Because some of them had relatives there. The questions became more intimate. "How old are you?" one woman asked Michelle. Her name was Olga, who looked to be in her fifties. She was obviously the head of the group. Michelle told her, twenty-three. "Oh my gosh, so old! Where are your children? You should have started having kids at least five years ago." The others laughed.

The chit-chat lasted a while. It reminded me of the porch conversations back in Tennessee, where people hung out and spent a Sunday afternoon together. These were country people, just like my father's own. And this was the deep countryside, far away from any city. The women talked amongst themselves for a long while, then turned to Magdalena to see what gossip she had to share. It was all about unwed mothers, drunken husbands, the priest who visited once a month to celebrate mass (they suspected he had a lover somewhere in a remote village). It lasted a while. Then, in a lull in the conversation, Olga turned to us, crossed her arms over her chest and said, "Well, I suppose it's time to get to work." She looked at Michelle, who had a pad and pen in hand. "Make sure you take good notes."

We were about to get into the plans for the delegation's arrival, setting dates and times and places to meet. But it wouldn't go that way. It couldn't. These women had their stories to tell, and they were going to make sure we heard them.

Olga began. "The Contras took my son, his name was... *is*, Juan Carlos. They came at night and rounded up all the teenage boys in the village and marched them into the woods. They forced them to join their ranks. But not until after they burned half our village down."

The other women had similar stories. It was the Contra strategy: enter a village, set it on fire, kill any man who came after them with a machete, shoot others who tried to run into the woods, and force the young men to follow them into the forest as new recruits. "They killed my husband. Slit his throat," one woman said, matter-of-factly, as though she had told this story many times before (which she had, with other delegations who had come through town). But as she continued, her voice shook slightly, not with fear or mourning, but anger.

After so many of the women shared their accounts of Contra attacks, Olga started talking politics. "You know," she said, "why this is all happening." She looked back and forth at Michelle and me. "Your president. Your government. They mean to kill us all off. Just like in Vietnam. But it's different—Reagan is smart. He won't send in your own military, but hires a mercenary group to do his bidding."

It was an intricate analysis of what was going on, not just in Nicaragua, but in the United States. They knew, through other delegations, that there were protests against Reagan's policies happening in the States, but it didn't seem like Washington, DC, was listening. There was a vote coming up in the Senate on whether or not to send one hundred million dollars to the Contras. The women knew there was a good chance of it passing.

It was impressive, how much they knew about US policy toward their country. Michelle asked how they kept up with all the news. Olga said, "Magdalena. She reads the newspapers to us, well, whenever the newspaper arrives here. It's always a week late. And Carmen has a radio." She pointed with her lips to a woman in the back pew, who nodded and smiled at us.

"I don't think the hundred million will pass," Michelle said. "There are too many protests going on back home to let that happen."

Olga chuckled. "You really believe that?" Then she gave more analysis: she returned to the Vietnam comparison. "In that war, your people protested hard, because US soldiers were getting killed. That's not the case here. It's Nicaraguan against Nicaraguan. Who cares what happens to us?" Now she sounded bitter.

One woman behind Olga said, shyly, "So, should we start planning on your friends coming here?"

Michelle picked up her pen and notepad. They started talking about dates of arrival, and how long the delegation would be with them. "Only one day," Michelle said, and mentioned how we had to go to another town called Quilalí, which was several miles east of Jícaro. "There's a refugee camp near there that we want to visit."

"I don't think that's a good idea," Magdalena said. She talked about skirmishes in the area between the warring sides.

Olga said it had cooled off in recent weeks. "Just be careful," she said. "Start out early, at daybreak. It's a long way there."

Chapter 18

The next day Magdalena fed us a hearty breakfast. It was early morning, still dark. She sent us off with a paper bag of tortillas and cheese. She was worried, but tried not to show it. "Just get back here before nightfall."

We got a ride on the back of a pickup truck, but the driver was going only a few miles out of town to check on his parcel of land. We had to walk most of the way. No cars drove by. We passed a few people, who waved at us as they walked along. They acted as though two gringos tromping through their territory was nothing special, though I'm sure we became dinner gossip once they returned home.

After about three hours of walking, we heard it: a battle had broken out between two ridges south of us. We could see it. Not the men who shot at the other ridge, but the tracer bullets, those red hot-glowing projectiles that showed the soldiers where to aim. They cut through the air from both sides. We were on a high ridge, and watched the shooting as though standing on a balcony.

There was a family who lived in a shack on the edge of the road. The father and mother had come out and were watching along with us. Two children ran out of the house. We made quick introductions, then stood there, looking, gauging. The battle was getting louder. It was moving our way.

"Oh shit," said the man. He looked at us and said that we might want to leave. Michelle agreed and asked if they had a place to go. While they nervously chatted, I made my way off the road and walked down the hill, toward the skirmish.

There was a certain, strange beauty to it. All those red tracer bullets zipping through the air between the two ridges, a mile or so below us. I walked a little closer. Michelle yelped, called out my name, screamed it really, and told me to get the fuck back up on the road. That meant she was really on the edge; she rarely uses the word *fuck*.

"I'm okay," I said. "I just want to see it a little more up close."

The arc of bullets moved closer to us. But a mile was more than plenty of space. Too much damn space, really. There was a singular thought in me: be there. See it from the inside. Maybe even pick up a rifle from a dead soldier and join the Sandinistas' ranks. It was lifting in my head, the wild effervescence that I had felt since high school, only now, it was peaking with the thought of joining a battle.

Michelle stomped off the road, walked up from behind, and snatched my arm. "Look!" she said, pointing to the shack. The family was gone. "*They left! They know to get out of the way!*" She pulled at me, and I followed her back to the road. I had to keep up with her as she trucked back toward Jícaro. She was right; I was clear-headed enough to see that I couldn't have joined the Sandinista forces; I would have been a hindrance. But I could have sat on a rock above the skirmish and watched until it ended.

She had scolded me, and that had brought me back, partly, to earth. As we walked on the road, she reminded me what the Witness for Peace trainers in Managua had taught us: as much as you can, stay out of harm's way. Which meant, I supposed, don't walk into a battle.

We never made it to Quilalí, but returned to Magdalena's house. A heaviness came over me. While Michelle and Magdalena drank coffee and talked outside, sitting on two old, rickety chairs, I lay down on the bed in the chicken coop room. I didn't sleep, but stared at a hen that was sitting on her eggs. It was the same pattern: the high of seeing the battle, to the inevitable drop afterwards. But the battle had lit something in me. I wanted more.

I had talked with soldiers about their experiences in the mountains and had pressed them on details. But most were too worn out with fighting, fasting for days, and fear. And I wanted *that*. I wanted to feel the chaos of battle, not knowing at the time that I was using the war as a tool to counterbalance the lifelong war in my head. Michelle, I thought, wasn't willing to go all the way, while I, electrified by revolution and risks, was ready to plunge. I felt a separation coming on. The delegation work pricked at me. My anger flared, "All those fucking delegates running around, it's embarrassing trucking a flock of gringos from one town to another!"

Our delegation was arriving soon. After setting up the meetings in Jícaro, we hitchhiked to Managua to greet them at the airport. I just knew, this one was going to do me in. The thought of riding the nice bus through the war zone with English-only-speaking gringos choked me. I wanted to hide in the zone, to be one with the people, to embed myself so much in Nicaraguan life no one could pry me out. I couldn't see the commitment in the eyes of the delegates, that they had shelled out money for the fact-finding tour, and that they would go back to their home states to preach the good word about the Sandinistas and the horrible word about the Contras. All I knew was, somehow, this latest delegation would break me.

Then Reagan intervened. He, who had helped bring Michelle and me together in college in our mutual loathing of the president and his foreign policies, now gave me the opportunity of not only missing the delegation, but also of seeing the war up close, more deeply than we had on the road, where the battle had approached us. It meant Michelle and I had to separate, which we had promised never to do.

The land mines were buried under a wide, flat plain between me and the Honduran border. I stood on the Nicaraguan side, about half a mile from Honduras. It was a foggy morning, thick with humidity. Though I couldn't see them, I knew the bombs were out there because of the sign next to me, *Peligro minas*—Danger mines. The Nicaraguan army must have put the sign up, to keep the locals out. They had nailed the message onto a stake and driven it into the ground. It was a brittle thing, half-cocked to one side, with the uneven black letters painted on the cracked board by a shaky hand. It looked like a warning that boys would make to keep the unwanted out of their treehouse, *No girls allowed!*

These were Nicaraguan bombs, sown into the ground to keep the enemy from invading. And the enemy was near. I could make them out beyond the scrub-less flatland. Their army personnel trucks rumbled on the far edge of the plain, over dirt roads at the foothills of the Honduran mountains.

The sun was rising. The fog lifted, enough for me to make out the trucks, which looked like toys in the distance. The mist still hung low in the chill air, just a few feet above my head. Desolation. As far as I could see, I was the only person out here, though a few men walked far behind me on the edge of a hamlet named Teotecacinte. They stepped into cornfields and disappeared among the stalks.

I had a shortwave radio in my backpack, and I pulled it out to listen to the morning news. Which newscast to tune in? Honduran radio stations no doubt parroted what Reagan had proclaimed the day before, that a brigade of the Sandinista army had invaded Honduras near Teotecacinte and was making its way toward the Honduran capital of Tegucigalpa. Here, where I stood alone, according to my president, battles raged.

I tried to tune in to a broadcast, but for a while all I could pick up was static. I couldn't find my favorite stations, Radio Habana out of Cuba and Radio Venceremos from El Salvador, both of them leftist programs. But even if I could, they wouldn't know what was happening—or rather, *not* happening—here. I was the only gringo in the area, and deeply disappointed. I had traveled here alone to witness a war, to see, firsthand and up close, the horror of battle. Nothing. I stood in the silence of a warless zone, tuning the radio. A station played early-morning marimba, indigenous music. It must have broadcast from Guatemala.

I kept tuning. An English voice cut through the static. It wasn't from American Forces Network, the official, international station of the US army, but an AM station from somewhere in the States. It was a talk show. The host sounded like a wannabee Rush Limbaugh. I listened while standing next to the *peligro minas* sign. He was talking over the phone to a conservative politician who spoke about the dire, violent, chaotic situation that was playing out right here, in one of the quietest places on earth. The host agreed, and started spouting off about the devilish Sandinistas.

The air above me must have shifted. The electrical current between the talk show and me turned another way. The static took over. I turned off the radio and shoved it into the backpack, then gazed at the plain.

There were no tiny buttons sticking out from under the ground. But there was a shimmer of energy lifting from the earth, all around me, in me.

The hamlet of Teotecacinte had woken up two hours before, with women rising long before dawn to make piles of tortillas for the day, just as they did in every village across Nicaragua, across Central America. Now, with the dawn, the roosters got to work. A hundred crowed in unison. Their *ki-kiri-kiris!* ran like a wave over the hamlet. Then silence. Then another wave, and another—they were the communal alarm clock.

More men left the hamlet, with machetes slung from their rope belts. They walked into corn fields. One farmer saw me. He waved, then yelled "¡Cuidado!" and headed my way. Suddenly I felt like a stupid child, with him telling me to be careful. He stopped about thirty feet from me, said good morning, and pointed to the sign. He asked if I knew what a mine was. I said yes and told him about the supposed Nicaraguan army incursion into Honduras. He looked confused. "No," he said, "we haven't had many problems here." Sometimes there were skirmishes, he said, but not too near Teotecacinte. He told me again to be careful, and that maybe I should step back from the sign. Such a kind voice, too kind, as though he were trying to hide what he really thought about me, something akin to, *You stupid fucking gringo.* "Good idea," I said. I fumbled with my backpack as though looking for car keys, and took a few steps toward Teotecacinte. The farmer smiled and went on his way. I waited until he entered the cornfield, then turned back to the sign.

Just one step in. The thought itself thrilled me. The nerve endings throughout my body popped with electricity. Lightning rose in me. Could the people of Teotecacinte hear the thunder bashing against the inside of my skull? I dropped the backpack on the ground, held the edge of the sign with my right fingers, stared at the earth behind it then stepped in.

Glory.

I stood there and slowly counted to ten, while studying the ground to see where to step next. I can feel it now, or rather, the echo of the rapture. I was fully myself—fully alive! Ten seconds of unbridled ecstasy. I took another step in, then a third, raised my face to the misty heavens, closed my eyes, breathed in the cool, morning Nicaraguan air, and opened my arms like Christ gesturing to the multitudes. I kept taking steps. The sign was about twenty feet behind me.

Once I turned and looked at it, reason came along and spoiled the moment, *I could explode!* Now I shook with fear. I stepped backwards out of the field, snatched the backpack and made to run back to the village. But I didn't. I stared at the plain. Breaths rattled out of me. The mania was rising.

*

Before my venture into the minefield, it had been a busy time in the Witness for Peace offices. They had three delegations coming in at once, one of them ours. We were short on staff. Because of Reagan proclaiming lies about an invasion, we had to send someone there to check it out. We had the strong suspicion that nothing was happening there. The Sandinistas had no reason to cross the border into Honduras. But we had to make sure.

Without a breath of hesitation, I had said, "I'll do it. I'll go." *I* will go. Not *we*. Michelle turned to me. The group was talking it over. Elizabeth, our boss, said she could pick up the slack on our delegation.

"What the hell?" Michelle said to me. "Why do *you* have to do it?"

"Everybody else is busy."

She knew how much I hated the delegations. She said that this was just a way of getting out of it. She argued with me—was I going to be stupid again and walk toward a battle? I said what the others had said, that this was probably another one of Reagan's lies.

The meeting broke up. I had to get ready to go north, because time was of the essence: supposedly that invasion was happening right now. I shoved toiletries, underwear, and the radio in my backpack while Michelle followed and berated me about putting myself in the middle of an invasion. She reminded me of our promise never to separate. I said, "I'll just go there and get back as quickly as I can." Then a thought came to me, "Hey, instead of coming back to Managua, why don't I meet you and the delegation in Jícaro?" That was a week away. It was a concession—if she'd let me go to the border, I would join up with her and work the delegation.

She knew, once I got this way, there was no talking me out of it. She shook her head, said "Okay," then made me promise that within the week, I would be in Jícaro.

The night after stepping into the minefield, I didn't sleep. Dawn came on. I was back in Ocotal, in the shitty hostel that had become one of our homes away from home. I had six days to get to Jícaro to meet up with Michelle.

I thought about going early, to spend time with Magdalena, but that wouldn't do—a man staying nights alone with a widow. That would cause rumors to fly. And I didn't have the energy. The very thought of hanging out with Magdalena, and getting into a deep conversation about all things revolutionary, wore me out. I dragged myself to a comedor, picked at a tamal, then dragged back to the hostel, where I spent the next days alone, not reading, not writing in my journal, just lying on the bed and staring at the stained ceiling. Finally, I bought a bottle of cheap whiskey and drank myself to sleep.

I believe martyrdom and suicide are cousins. I remember thinking, while standing on the edge of the minefield, *If I die here, they might end the war.* My death could help the cause. I believed it; I wanted it, up until the moment that I didn't. As much as I had delved into another people's war, I couldn't conceal the battles in my head. Suicide by martyrdom. My death would have purpose. Now, holed up in the hostel, I shook with fear.

Days later I hitchhiked to Jícaro. The delegation was already there. Michelle was more elated than angry. She greeted me with a solid hug and a long kiss. Magdalena told me what a brave man I was, to report on an invasion, no matter that it didn't happen. We all went to a comedor for lunch. Michelle said, her voice low and pissed, "We're *not* going to separate anymore." She looked at me with those hazel eyes that, in certain moments, turn hard as steel. Then she squeezed my hand and kissed my cheek. I didn't tell her about the land mines.

I promised myself to never do such a thing again. The mania that had gotten me to walk into the minefield had been too much. The electricity still shot through my nerves. The lack of sleep was working on me—the first sign of a manic attack and possible breakdown. But I didn't break down. I just shivered with it all—the mines, and the separation from Michelle. A week without her at my side. I had broken a promise. Guilt, yes, but also the recognition that I needed her more than I realized.

We sat with the delegation, ate, drank beer, with reggae music playing on a radio in the background. It was festive. I liked the delegates, got into some good chats with them, enough for me to forget my nerves for as long as the conversation lasted. Magdalena and a half-dozen other Nicaraguans ate with us. Michelle and I translated the conversations. Because of the minefield and the subsequent days of solitude in the hostel, the delegation work suddenly took on meaning. Michelle was right—this was a major part of our mission.

I, twenty-three, had no vocabulary for what was happening in my brain. Nor did I recognize that a Latino-gringo can go only so far when it comes to finding one's roots. You may go deep, but you'll never be able to go fully native. I might have felt this at the time, but, as with the sickness, I couldn't articulate it. All I knew that day, when we rendezvoused in Jícaro, was that it didn't bother me, at all, to be with a group of fellow US citizens. I didn't mind speaking English with them, and I joined alongside Michelle in hosting them through our section of the war zone.

We saw no action. We returned, unscathed, to Managua, sent the folks off on their flights home, and took a couple of days in the Witness for Peace house to rest. Afterwards Michelle said, "Okay, time to go back, don't you think?" Back to Jícaro, back to traveling from one village to another, on dirt roads, under a blistering sun or through rain that soaked you to the soul. I was in bed, mute. She asked, "Are you okay?"

"I'm just tired. Can we stay maybe another night?"

We did. She slept. I lay beside her and stared at the beams in the ceiling until dawn. The next day, we trekked north, back to the war zone.

Chapter 19

They had killed all the rabid dogs before we arrived. The five carcasses were scattered across the settlement, in between the refugees' huts. The Sandinista soldiers had shot them that morning. The captain had ordered the refugees to stay away from the dogs until the next day, to keep from getting infected.

According to the captain, the hounds had stumbled out of the forest at dawn. They were starving and had followed the scent of food into the camp. A few had had foam dripping from their jaws.

The refugees and soldiers had built the camp in a meadow surrounded by hillocks. It was a beautiful place, with a thick forest that encircled the site. It looked akin to the mountains of Tennessee. But the camp itself was an eyesore. They had built their shacks with pruned branches covered in black plastic. The refugees had dug latrines between the tiny houses, with no walls, only the plastic hanging off the sticks for privacy. The swarms of flies around the outhouses buzzed mercilessly and shone green and black in the rays of a ruthless Nicaraguan sun.

A patrol of green-clad Sandinista soldiers guarded the camp, smoking, chatting, with their AK-47 rifles hanging from their shoulders. They didn't seem worried. The captain, a solid and slender man, maybe thirty years old, said that there were no enemy troops in the area. Some of the soldiers walked among the shacks. They chatted with refugee men. One soldier and a few civilians were smoking near a Jeep. They talked about everyday things: the weather; a deer that some men, with their own rusted rifles, had hunted yesterday; the sacks of rationed beans that finally arrived from Managua; the children who played between the shacks; and the dead and scattered dogs.

This was the camp that Michelle and I had tried to reach a few weeks earlier, when we came across the battle on the way to Quilalí. It was a new settlement of around a hundred poor farmers and their families. They were from a cluster of hamlets thirty kilometers to the north, near the Honduran border. They were not happy. It had been an abrupt move, with all of them uprooted from their homes in one night when a battle had neared their community. They had lived in the camp for a month, long enough to shake off the panic of the escape, build the shacks, dig the holes for the latrines, arrange stones in circles on the ground to burn wood for cooking, take inventory of the few possessions they managed to carry with them, and fall into a deep and communal sadness about their adobe houses that had no doubt been reduced to rubble.

Michelle was dressed in a long skirt that reached her ankles. Her white plastic slippers were scratched and stained from so much walking through the country. It was a blue skirt, I believe. And her blouse, white? With red roses embroidered on the neckline? My illness resurges as I write this. I see Michelle's beauty, which is a mistake. Michelle had lost weight she couldn't afford to lose. Her cheeks looked like miniature scaffolds of bones, covered with tarps of dried skin. She had suffered from amoebas during our time in the country. Vomiting, daily diarrhea, the cramps made by worms that wallowed in her gut. But in memory I still see her as beautiful.

We had visited other refugee settlements without having to ask for permission. The camps were open. The refugees could leave if they wanted to. But there was nowhere for them to go. The settlement was the only safe place in the territory. Michelle and I had to write an account on why the Sandinistas had ordered the civilians to leave their homes in a nighttime move. According to Reagan, the Sandinistas, for no reason, had forced their own people into "concentration camps." We visited to interview refugees about the situation and write a report from their testimonials, which would be sent to the Witness for Peace office in Washington, DC.

We asked the captain if we could speak with a few people. He nodded his head and said, "Talk to whoever you want." We thanked him and shook hands.

Michelle looked at a woman who was squatting over a fire circle in front of her hut. She said, "Let's start with her." The captain squinted and looked at the undergrowth below his feet, as though regretting giving us permission. He walked to his Jeep.

The woman in the hut was pissed. She used more swear words than verbs. She hated the Sandinistas and said it to each soldier who passed by. She dared the young men to shut her up. They walked on, ignoring her taunts.

She was around forty years old and solid as a boulder. Her name was Rosalba. She stayed squatted over a cauldron on the low fire, stirring a soup made out of water and roots she'd dug out of the forest. She gave us a half-baked welcome, and invited us to her home, "humble as it is," and added that "our visit was a joy." She said that without much joy.

A little boy sat on a stool in the black plastic shack. Rosalba told him to give it to Michelle. I sat on a stump.

The Sandinista assholes. The bastard soldiers. The fucked-up captain. Her abandoned house in a new motherfucking war zone, a home that no longer existed, not after the sons of a bitch of both armies shot their mortars into the hamlet. Rosalba said it all in a voice that could tear a tank to pieces.

She served us coffee in blue, scratched plastic cups. Michelle accepted it with a smile and a "thank you very much," but she didn't drink it. She didn't risk any drink. She had suffered from dysentery for a week. After a regimen of Flagil—a medicine that nearly rips your guts out while killing the amoebas—she wasn't taking on any more risks. Rosalba could have boiled the water until it steamed, and Michelle wouldn't even have inhaled it.

The cups were filled with lukewarm water, with a spoonful of the government-rationed coffee mixed with roasted ground corn. At that moment, it began. The first sip roused the wild demon that had been unleashed in the minefield. Warm coffee, with a temperature that wouldn't kill a fly, much less an amoeba.

When Rosalba looked down at her root soup, Michelle gave a sharp flick of her mug, her wrist a pure whip, and sprayed the undergrowth behind her with coffee.

Before Rosalba could launch another volley of curses, I asked, "Excuse me, ma'am, where does your water come from? There's no river or lake around here."

She said, while stirring the broth and without looking at me, "Down there, from that well." She pointed to it Nicaraguan-style: with her protruding lips. "The Sandinistas dug it out before we arrived. It's the only thing that's worth anything in this fucking place."

A well. I calmed down. I didn't need to worry. The water, born from deep under the earth, was clean. Then I saw the dead dog. All the corpses of the other animals disappeared from my sight. This sole dog, near the well, was mine. Or, I was his.

The carcass was about fifty feet away from the well, which was covered with a large, round, wooden plug, made by the hands of a skilled carpenter. No cracks, not even a mosquito could have penetrated it. But there was the dog lying on the ground, as if sleeping, with a bullet hole in its flank. A dog that, that morning, had prowled the settlement with the dribble of hot bubbles dripping from its jaw.

It began. And now, as I write, it begins again, as if the concept of Time has never existed. I am once again in the refugee camp. Something is snapping in my mind. Something is pushing out from inside my head, the thing that I had locked down all my life. It threatens to crack through the bone of my skull. I see things that no one else can see: A transparent but thick, living mist covers the whole settlement. The refugees and soldiers walk on the other side of the haze that is, for them, invisible. They can pass between the curtains of the cloud, curtains that do not open for me. Rosalba squats over the fire and the pot, and keeps stirring. She and Michelle talk about . . . something . . . Their words push against my mist, like whispers against a pillow. From inside here, all of out there becomes unreal. Michelle, Rosalba, the soldiers, the refugees, and their children that run between the huts are strange, foreign. The mist creates a hermetic solitude, but I'm not alone. The dog is with me.

The dog is dead. That means the rabies is dead too, right? But how long can the virus survive? The soldiers killed all the dogs at dawn. Now it's three in the afternoon. At least nine hours have passed. But a virus is a stubborn animal. It can live in the clots of dried blood, I'm sure, very sure. The blood melts in the afternoon heat and mixes with the foam in the dog's mouth, making a broth of madness, which drips and splashes onto the ground.

The rabies soaks the earth, soaks the undergrowth under the dog's jaw and passes like mercury through the clay. It breaks through bedrock then suddenly turns toward the well and pierces the wall of the deep hole, mixes with the water that I have just sipped. The rabies is inside me, where it waits, where it has waited since childhood.

Chapter 20

Just before we left Nicaragua, Michelle suffered her own panic attack. She was sure that we would die on the dusty road in the mountains. We traveled in the bed of an open truck that was once used to transport cows. The cattle farmer had become a taxi driver, and he crammed the truck bed with more than thirty men, women, children, all of us standing and pressed against each other. Many carried bags of corn, fruit, and live chickens that they planned to sell to markets in Ocotal. They were also afraid, rightly so. There could have been mortars in the road, planted there by the Contras.

I wasn't afraid. The sadness over our departure from Nicaragua shielded me from the strange terror that had overwhelmed me in the refugee settlement. I didn't want to leave. I wanted to live the rest of my life in Central America, and move to El Salvador. I hated Reagan. I hated Washington, DC. for its long history of US invasions in Latin America, and I loathed the American people for their apathy. But the anger barely covered the pain of longing that thrummed in my chest—to be Salvadoran, to be completely Latino.

We all stood, tight as sardines in a can. A poor farmer, skinny, somewhere in his thirties, told us colorful jokes. He was a good storyteller, and he distracted the riders from the fear over road bombs. A pregnant woman said that even her baby inside was laughing. The storyteller pulled an orange out of a brown plastic bag, peeled it, tore apart the wedges, and handed the pieces to the people around him, leaving one for himself, and kept telling stories.

Each time the driver took a sudden turn on the road, to dodge a rock that looked like a mortar button, Michelle pressed her eyes closed, waiting, praying that we would return to our families alive. Others crossed themselves and murmured trembling prayers. It was dawn. I looked at the mountains around us, ate the orange wedge, and tried to hide my tears. I didn't think about dead dogs or lukewarm coffee or rabid wells, not even about mortars or ambushes of enemy troops. My mind was occupied with a cascade of considerations: Could we return to Central America? Or should we continue on with our previous lives in the States? This made me shudder. Everything, *everything*, had changed. We were not the same people who had left the States nearly a year ago.

Our return to the United States, along with worries about our future in the States—finding employment, deciding where to live—put a plug on the rabies hallucination in the refugee camp. We stayed with Mamá in Tennessee until we could find work. I wanted to talk to her only in Spanish, which pleased her to no end.

But it didn't take long. In Tennessee, the sadness swallowed me. Just like past episodes (in those days we did not call them episodes; we had no word to define the extreme changes of my moods), I fell into the hollow of an erratic, horrifying depression. There, the dog was waiting for me.

I see them in memory, my wife and mother, looking at me while I screamed, in English, about the dead dog, about the cup of virus that I had sipped, and that I was going to die of rabies within a few days. My cries and whimpers frightened them. Did they see me as insane, or was I convincing them? I babbled my certainties, that soon the hot foam would fall from my mouth, my eyes would fill with blood, the barking would burst out of my infected lungs, and the rabies would take over my mind.

They took me to a doctor, who explained to me, in a soft, Appalachian voice, that a well can't give you rabies, and that the dog was so far away from the well, there was no way it could have infected the water. I calmed down for a few hours, but the terror returned. *I've got rabies oh God!* Michelle didn't know what to say. I frightened them both. Suddenly Mamá said, desperately, "Well, if it kills you, at least you won't suffer the rabies anymore."

That statement, for another son, would have been cruel. Cold. But for me, she spoke with a certain common sense. It calmed me for a while, though the image of the dog at the well still pricked at my mind. It still does, especially when stress rouses childhood and childhood sets off the illness. Some days the dog is very close. Other times it wanders away, as though to give me a reprieve. But when it's near, it growls at me while running through the twists and turns of this skull, rattling its own head, flinging the bloody, boiling foam that splashes into every corner of my brain.

I didn't understand that the abuse in childhood was leaking up through the floor of my subconscious—not memory (for I had always remembered), but poison. All I believed was that I carried the rabies virus and feared the day when it would manifest, when foam would pour out of my mouth.

But I fought it. Pressed it down as best I could. We still had work to do for the Nicaraguan cause. We joined the Witness for Peace circuit for three months, giving lectures on our experiences. Afterwards we found jobs at an environmental education camp in the Smoky Mountains, called Wesley Woods.

I didn't want this at first, didn't want to return to Appalachia. The time in Nicaragua, I wanted to believe, had shaken my white culture out of me. All I wanted was to speak Spanish daily, and live amongst fellow Latinos, who were nowhere to be found in east Tennessee.

But those two years in the Smoky Mountains were just what we needed. We lived in a cabin at the base of the camp's mountain, small, isolated, sitting in a field next to a horse stable and farm. We owned no television and got all our news from NPR. The cabin was heated by a wood-burning stove that sat in the middle of the house, which meant I had to start cutting firewood in the summer to prepare for winter. I split wood and stacked the pieces into a long cord that reached the height of my waist.

The cabin was the perfect size for a couple, with two bedrooms (one of them became my office; I started a novel about a country in revolution), a bathroom with a tub for bathing (no shower), and a small kitchen with a gas stove. We had a cat named Chigüina, a Nicaraguan word for "child." Whenever I came through the front door, Chigüina, who was sitting on the top of the refrigerator, would leap onto my shoulders and curl around my neck. I'd carry him that way through the house, wearing him like a mink stole.

The people we worked with on the seven-hundred-acre camp were good, evangelical folks who never cursed and, surprisingly, didn't foist upon us their love of Jesus. They even forgave us our Catholicism, though they were curious about the strange ways of our church, such as baptizing babies, pouring the holy water just on their foreheads, unlike their religion, where an adult got a full dunking in a river. They didn't smoke or drink. They were from these mountains, from deep inside the folds of ridges. Some of the kindest people I have known.

It was a bucolic time. A tranquil time. We worked with school kids who came in by the busloads to spend a week in the woods. We taught environmental education, the dangers of climate change, and arts and crafts. But most of the work was physical. We had those kids do things that would shake a mother to her knees: rock climbing, spelunking, and climbing up twenty feet into trees that had high ropes tied between them, which they walked on, with thick mountain climbing ropes hitched to their hips to keep them from hitting the ground. We took them on miles-long hikes through the giant camp, walking the kids through grand coves and valleys, for hours.

It was, in retrospect, my asylum. The physical labor was good for me. We lived in nature, far from any town. And I'm talking nature: once, while sitting at my writing desk, I looked out the window and watched a huge black bear gallop across the field.

The disconnect from the world was good for my brain. The physical labor kept the demons at bay. It helped shake out of me the image of the rabid dog, though that dog still appeared from time to time. But it didn't have the same power as before. It was the setting itself that calmed me. I now imagine the asylums of old, where a psychologically ill person could go to get away, far away from the harsh, obstreperous world that had driven him into madness. The good asylums had gardens for the sick to wander around in. I had my own garden, seven hundred acres of it. Wesley Woods became my own personal sanctuary.

We had settled in. We also continued to be involved in the Central American struggle. In Knoxville, about thirty minutes away, we joined with the local Unitarian Church, which had set up a sanctuary for refugees who had fled the violence in El Salvador and Guatemala. A young Guatemalan couple named Carlos and Juanita, along with their two kids, lived in the basement of the church. We became friends. None of the Unitarians spoke Spanish, so Michelle and I acted as translators. We also spent hours with the couple in their makeshift apartment, talking in Spanish about all things, from their two little boys to their escape from death squads in their home country. The talks kept me plugged into myself, into my need to go all-out Latino.

There was a group of activists in the South who had created "The Overground Railroad." Rather than hiding refugees in churches, these folks drove them from the Texas border all the way to Canada, where they accepted Central Americans. Our part of the trek was to take the refugees from a small commune in Georgia, to the town of Berea, Kentucky, where another driver waited to take them the rest of the way.

We drove entire families through the mountains, staying away from interstates and taking county roads. I remember one family who had three children, all under the age of ten. Once we reached the peak of Clingmans Dome, the highest point of the Smoky Mountains, we were driving in snow, something the family had never seen. I stopped the car. The kids ran out in it and opened their mouths to catch the flakes. I thought about my mother, who had told me that back in the winter of 1947, when Dad had brought her home on the Harley, she had done the same thing, trying to catch the snow on her tongue.

These people kept Michelle and me connected to Central America. They helped me stay on the road to my own latinidad. We were fluent in Spanish. I still studied vocabulary, every day, and read aloud from Spanish books. By then, I had discovered the Chilean poet Pablo Neruda, and I read him like an evangelical studying a Bible. I also had a copy of the Nicaraguan poet Gioconda Belli's collection *Mi íntima multitud*, which helped keep me connected to our lives there.

In retrospect, it seems rather strange: I was living in both my cultures and was comfortable in both. The locals had shown me a face of Appalachia that I had not known in childhood. The refugees who became our friends kept us plugged into our lives in Central America.

But it wasn't enough, for either of us. We had learned about a Catholic organization named Maryknoll that worked in Central America, and we hoped to someday join it, to return to the old countries, maybe El Salvador. Then Michelle became pregnant, and our focus changed—it lit up in her the desire to be a mom. I would be a father, and that thought pleased me, though it didn't quell my desire to return to Central America; we'd just bring the baby along. He or she would grow up in a Latino world.

Unfortunately, Michelle miscarried, which sent her into her own spiral of depression. For weeks she mourned. It was then that I saw, for the first time, the mother in her, the desire to have children. She kept working, but there was a heaviness to it all. I worried that she was falling into her own depression. Which she was.

Then, after a while, she picked herself up and dove more deeply into our work, both in the environmental education camp and with the refugees. That was her way—to get back to living. It's one of the strengths in her that I have, through the years, come to rely on. She spoke more about going overseas. She was ready to move on as much as I.

After two years of living in the woods, two years that had given me time, space, and physical labor to heal my mind, we left and made our way back to Central America.

Chapter 21

Maryknoll was a home-grown, Catholic, US missionary organization that served all over the struggling world. It had been in the South Americas for decades. Maryknoll had a name in Central America, in one person's mouth, praise, in another, condemnation. They were seen by some as a leftist group, communist-leaning, and were no longer allowed to go into El Salvador. This disappointed me. I was hoping we would get assigned to my mother's home country.

We were sent to Guatemala instead. Unlike Nicaragua, which was liberated, Guatemala still lived under a military-backed regime. Any positive whispers about the Nicaraguan revolution could get a Guatemalan killed for being a communist. There was violence, tremendous violence. And yet, I see the country as one of the most beautiful I've ever been in, with a people that are like no other on the planet. I think about Guatemala near-daily; moments from thirty years ago shoot through me, and they're not all bad, they're not just about the oppression. I see faces: Joaquín Che' Ax, his wife María, Chamba Cutzál, Delia Chicmúl. For some, Spanish was their second language. Most spoke in Mayan.

There are twenty-three languages in the country, one of them Spanish. The rest are not dialects of a specific Mayan tongue, but are as distinct from one another as French is from German: Q'eqchi', Ch'ol, Tzotzil, K'iche', to name a few. As is their clothing. Their weaves are in themselves holy, in a way that I, an outsider, couldn't fully understand—colorful weaves that represent each Mayan community throughout the country. In the Petén, the northern jungle of the nation, the women wore ankle-length, wraparound skirts that were a greenish gold. Their embroidered *huipiles*—blouses—were multicolored works of art.

We worked with a priest, Father Chamba Cutzal. He was a stout man, my height, with oak-colored skin and an undoubtedly Mayan-indigenous face. His first language was Spanish, but he tended to lean more to his Mayan roots, preferring to speak Q'eqchi', sometimes dressing in indigenous clothing, and participating in ceremonies that dated back hundreds of years before Jesus.

Joaquín Che' Ax was our gardener. He and his wife María volunteered for the parish, and helped Michelle and me in our work. María made sure tamales and hot chocolate were always served at our adult education classes. I see other faces of the people we worked with, a mix of indigenous and mestizo, and though I don't remember all their names, I feel them. They taught us a different life, one that we couldn't slip into, not completely. Time, land, weather, crops, births, deaths, marriages, the preparation of food, all had a sense of the otherworldly about it, much like the world of *One Hundred Years of Solitude*.

All those people. But two stand out from the crowd, two babies who made radical changes in our life: Lazarito and Raquel.

Before we met those two children, we had been in Guatemala about eight months, living in Poptún, a town in the north, in the middle of the jungle. Our job was to facilitate community meetings about everything from the Catholic Church's seven sacraments to land issues, the basic issue being that the people had no land. All of it was owned by wealthy Guatemalans in faraway places, such as Miami: thousands upon thousands of acres under one name. We tried to figure out in our meetings how the landless could buy small parcels of it together to form a cooperative, everyone chipping in to purchase an acre or two, on which they would plant a communal crop of corn. Such ways of thinking were suspect. They were also reported to the military—there were, Father Chamba told us, *orejas*, or "ears" in every meeting, men the army paid to report on groups such as ours.

It didn't take Chamba long to become more intimate with us. At first, he addressed us as *usted*, but once we told him about our time in Nicaragua, his eyes brightened. He smiled. He left *usted* behind, jumped over the familiarity of *tú* and went directly to addressing us intimately as *vos*.

Sometimes it was hard to tell that Chamba was a priest. He said mass, listened to confessions, and administered the sacraments. But he was about Liberation Theology more than any of us, and he didn't call it Liberation Theology, just *la lucha*, the struggle. Some of his family had been murdered by the military. I asked him once, why did he become a priest? "I had two choices. Either join the guerrillas or the priesthood. I'm practically blind," he motioned to his glasses. "I'd be worth shit in the woods. So I decided to fight from the inside."

Fight. He meant revolution. But here, in Guatemala, that word could get a man tortured or killed or both. In Nicaragua, our conversations got loud whenever talking about la lucha. Here, we had to watch our words and the pitch of our voices. Whenever talking about *la situación*, we spoke in murmurs. We were living in one of the most oppressed, violent nations on the planet. Death squads were as common as in El Salvador. The military's special forces, called Los Kaibiles, had their training camp on the edge of town. On the front of their building hung a large banner with a skull and crossbones, a huge knife clutched in the skull's teeth, and the words *persígnate antes de entrar* underneath. "Cross yourself before entering." As though the Kaibil camp were a dark church.

Chamba was not from Poptún. His Mayan language, Q'achiquel, was not the same, at all, as Q'eqchi'. He was born in the mountains of Chimaltenango, in the south, where the nickname for Guatemala—*The land of eternal springtime*—made sense. Here, in the town of Poptún, smack in the middle of the jungle, it was the land of eternal perspiration. We sweated like farm animals. We were in an outpost of Guatemalan society, the Appalachia of the country, cut off from the rest of the nation, distant, forgotten. Soldiers walked the streets. They were nothing like the Sandinistas. People did not talk with them and certainly wouldn't dare argue or raise their voices or even look them in the eye. They were better equipped than the Sandinistas, with belts of grenades around their waists, nine-millimeter parabellum pistols in holsters and US-made M16 machine guns slung over their shoulders. Father Chamba taught us, better to just walk on and don't give them the eye. Don't say hello to them, don't smile at them. Pretend, not that they don't exist, but you don't.

We had come to Poptún during a time when Chamba was going through his own personal metamorphosis. He was a priest and performed all the sacraments dutifully. He visited the sick and led community meetings in faraway villages. He learned the local Q'eqchi'. During the day, he worked with his fellow Mayans and at night plowed through a grammar book and a Q'eqchi'-Spanish dictionary. On his desk he had books on Mayan history, sociology, and philosophy. He carried around a copy of the *Popul Vu*, the Mayan "bible" that had been written down centuries ago, a book that had many gods and explained the birth of creation through jaguars, rabbits, turtles, and capricious deities.

Chamba had a hunger to know his own culture. Though born in the Mayan world and raised in two languages—Spanish and Q'achiquel—eight years in the seminary had Europeanized him. Taking on Christian studies had meant tearing away from his indigenous roots. He learned teachings that were from far away, theologies in which there is only one god. He was ordained young, in his mid-twenties. I don't know how fervent he was in the first years of his priesthood, but by the time we came along, he was questioning it. He wanted to throw himself completely into the Mayan world, as though to make up for the years of losing it.

He craved his culture as much as I craved mine, maybe even more. He tied together his own personal search with the struggle of the people. This teaching has stayed with me. In my own journey to my roots, I learned from him that you can't do it alone. You can't do it just for yourself. He taught me that to be Latino means to be *decidido*, to stand up for human rights. The search for oneself and the decision to stand for the poor and oppressed are inextricable.

*

We had jobs as teachers in an adult education program run by the church. We had one town to live in, rather than tramping from one village to another as we had in Nicaragua. We could put some roots down here. We rented a small adobe house, got to know our neighbors, and bought fresh tortillas every day from Doña Marta who lived next door.

We did missionary things, such as visiting the sick, bringing communion to the bedridden, and meeting with the men and women who were involved in the land cooperative. We spent a lot of time on rickety front porches, talking with folks about anything that came to mind, much like the porch-sits back in Tennessee.

Here, we had a schedule: morning coffee and sweet breads. Buying groceries at the local open market. Washing our clothes in a *pila*, a large cement washboard with a sink. We saw the same people every day. We didn't live out of backpacks and never had to jump on the bed of a cattle truck for a ride, as we had our own Jeep.

It was a stable life, which I needed, though at the time I didn't know why. I didn't know about the sickness, and that one of the ways to keep the illness at bay is to have a certain order in your days, predictable, repetitive. As in Wesley Woods, the rhythm soothed me, kept me on a certain balance, and made work not only easier, but more enjoyable.

When we had first arrived, Chamba had acted as our tour guide. He had been organizing long before we'd gotten there, and had run the community meetings on his own. Our job was to take his place in town, so he could spend more time in outlying villages, where he celebrated mass, baptized babies, married young couples and met with the locals to organize. His idea was to have both townspeople and country folk working for the same goal: land distribution. Just small parcels, not enough to raise too much attention from the authorities.

After taking us from one barrio to another—we met no less than a dozen people that day—he had seen the weariness in our faces and said it was time for a beer and a meal. But instead of taking us to a local comedor in Poptún, he drove us out to a farm in the middle of the woods, a property owned by Mike and Carole DeVine, two expats who had left the United States years ago. The DeVines hadn't come to farm, but to start a jungle bed and breakfast for people passing through to see the temples of Tikal. They had built a number of cabins and had set up a dining room that could seat fifteen people at a time. The tourists came mostly from Europe. Most of them, young, adventurous, had no real idea what was happening in the country. They lived out of backpacks. And they were all white, which was strange, to find a camp of Caucasians in the middle of a Mayan world.

Mike DeVine was a veteran of the Vietnam War. He was from Iowa. He and Michelle connected on that one. He was a tall man with a thick auburn beard and soft eyes. Carole, much shorter, had a welcoming smile for everyone who walked through the door.

They were a nice couple, but I didn't want to see them much. We hadn't come to Guatemala to hang out with gringos. I wanted to avoid them as I had avoided most of the delegation work in Nicaragua. Life was still all about finding my latinidad. The more I walked the road into Central America, the further away I believed the past became. By plunging into my Latino side, I was distancing myself from the horrors of childhood. I was still deep in the *Fuck the past* way of thinking, as though slamming the door on my childhood. Nothing but the present and the future for me. But when it came to such notions of time, the Guatemalans showed me that there were other ways of considering it. Ways that were strange, disturbing, and true.

One Saturday, during our adult education class, Michelle, an artist, had drawn a detailed timeline on a large roll of paper that we hung on the wall. It strung out from one corner to the next. She had painted pictures of the major events in Christian history, from Adam and Eve, to King David, to the birth of Christ, the crucifixion, the apostles, Martin Luther's split from the Catholic Church, all the way to the Second Vatican Council of the 1960s.

As the people walked in and greeted us, they looked at the timeline, confused. They saw the images, one after another, which made no sense to them. I didn't know this until I started teaching the history of the Church throughout the ages. I began with Adam and Eve and worked my way from left to right, pointing out the different, significant moments of Judeo-Christian history. At one point, I looked at the crowd and saw that it wasn't sinking in.

It was Joaquín Che' Ax, my gardener, who stood up and asked, "Excuse me Don Marcos, but, what the hell is that thing?"

"It's a timeline."

They muttered. *A what? A timeline. What's that? I don't know. Why's he walking left to right? Why is Jesus to the right of King David? Why is the resurrection to the left of the Apostles?*

I said again that it was a timeline, "You know, a way of measuring time."

Measuring time. That just made them more confused. I started again, from left to right, "See, how one thing leads to another?" I touched the drawings of the timeline with my fingertips. "The things on the left are in the past. Then they move forward, into the future, into our own time." I smiled, having explained it so very clearly.

They stared at me as though I were the strangest man on earth. After a few more attempts to get into their heads the concept of a timeline, I asked them, how did they measure time? They didn't answer. "What I mean is, how do you remember when things happened in the past?"

They turned to one another and started talking about corn crops. The seasons. How one winter a few years back was the wettest they'd ever seen. How a drought had once dried up much of the crops, and no doubt another drought was in their future, because that's how things go: in a circle.

That made absolutely no sense to me. There was no accuracy to it. I asked, "How in the world do you all keep up with birthdays?"

Some laughed at that. They talked with one another about their ages. "How old are you, María?"

"I think around thirty-five."

Her husband Joaquín laughed, "You liar, you're closer to forty and you know it."

Delia Chicmúl said to Joaquín, "I don't know how old you are, cousin, but you're getting way up there."

They guessed others' ages. One man was somewhere between forty and forty-five, another was more accurate: between thirty and thirty-two. Then they tired of it, as though knowing one's age really wasn't that important to everyday life.

I was still looking for accuracy. "How do you keep up with the days? How do you know when to come to the meetings?"

Joaquín said, "We've got a calendar at home."

"A calendar moves from left to right," I said.

"What?"

"The days. One after the other. In a line."

"Sorry Marcos, but you're not making any sense."

We continued on with the meeting. They obliged me, following along as I moved from left to right on the timeline. It was hard to focus. The conversation had disturbed me. Time as circular, not linear. Time as a round thing, one that came back upon itself. It meant that all things came back around. All.

After the meeting, Michelle and I went home. I wrote in my journal, in Spanish, about life in Poptún, our work, the people. Inevitably the writing turned inward. The questions came on again, *What is happening? Why do I feel this way? What set it off?* The Saturday class had thrown me into the old fears—the past, according to the Mayans, is not a distant thing, but something that circles around, over and again. But at the moment, I wasn't thinking about time lines or round notions of history. All I knew was that my mind was slipping, once again, into the jagged moods.

Chapter 22

Something was happening in our marriage, and it took me a while to catch on to what it was. We were twenty-six and had been married four years. Once we got settled in Poptún, it came over her: Michelle became, for lack of better word, rapacious in bed. I didn't complain. I didn't know that something was emerging out of her, and it wasn't going away anytime soon.

It took some time, but after several months of living there, she started throwing up in the mornings. Word got out. It was exciting, the notion that a gringa was going to give birth here. They were proud, as though the pregnancy were theirs as much as it was ours, which, in communal Guatemalan terms, it was. So happy were they with the notion, they forgave us our gringo ways, such as rushing to the capital of Guatemala City for prenatal care, instead of visiting the local, squalid clinic.

In the capital, we met with a doctor who had been trained in the States. He had a nice, air-conditioned office. Bach played on a cassette in the waiting room. We were worried, because of the miscarriage in Tennessee. He said that worry wasn't worth a thing, that all it did was put more stress on the mother and child. "And you want to avoid stress as much as possible." He asked us where we lived.

"Poptún," I said.

He was writing something down, but jerked his head up to us. "You live in *Poptún*?" He cringed slightly. "Well, try your best."

*

After we met with the doctor, we spent the night in the Maryknoll Center House in Guatemala City. It was a reprieve from the life in the jungle, with hot water, a large first-world kitchen, private rooms, and three square meals a day brought to us by servants. Priests lived there, some of them retired, others who were passing through.

Sister Dianna Ortiz was a Mexican American nun who had moved to Guatemala to teach literacy classes in far-off villages. She was young, perhaps our age. We had never met her before. She was attending a retreat in the small colonial town of Antigua, an hour outside of the capital. The day we had our appointment with the doctor, Dianna disappeared.

A squad of civilian-dressed men had kidnapped her, had taken her to a warehouse, and tortured her. They accused her of being a communist. They tied her down and burned her over a hundred times with cigarettes. They gang raped her.

Twenty-four hours after her abduction, another man had come in, white, with long brown hair and sunglasses. He screamed at the torturers, "Idiots! Leave her alone. She's a North American, and it's all over the news!"

He took her away in a Jeep. While driving, he spoke to Dianna in perfect English, "I'm sorry, this was all a mistake, they confused you with someone else. You're okay now. I'm going to take you to the US Embassy, they'll take care of you." Dianna, broken, burnt, raped, jumped out of the Jeep when he came to a red light and ran into the city's central market. She was Mexican American; she blended in; she escaped. She called the Maryknoll offices. A priest named Clarence found her and brought her to the house.

Outside, a regiment of soldiers surrounded the house. They demanded that we release Dianna, that they needed to take her in for questioning. The Maryknoll priests locked and barred the tall steel gate. Military officials called. The priests refused. The officials threatened them. And still the priests refused. Father Clarence not only said no, but reminded them what it would look like to have an American missionary murdered by death squads in Guatemala.

The military surrounded us for two days. Father Clarence called every source he could think of, including Amnesty International. He called the bishop of the Guatemala City Diocese, who called a cardinal, who called the pope. One of John Paul II's servants of the Lord had been tortured, and now she was in danger of being killed. He sent word to the Papal nuncio, who was the pope's right-hand man in Central America and, in retrospect, one of the bravest people I have seen. The Papal nuncio pulled up to the Maryknoll house in his limousine, stood outside, berated the soldiers for their actions, demanded to talk with the one in charge, and gave him a good tongue whipping as only a Catholic priest in Guatemala can do. "¡Aléjense!" he yelled at the soldiers who stood at the front gate, *Back off!* They obeyed. He had his chauffeur drive into the compound. He walked into the house and smiled at Dianna, took her hand, and shepherded her to the limousine. They drove to the airport. The Papal nuncio walked her all the way to the plane, with soldiers following right behind him. He sat her in first class. The plane took her home, where her community of nuns would spend the next decades helping her heal.

Once the soldiers left us alone, Michelle and I returned to Poptún. She began to bleed. Neighbors came. They offered all their remedies to stop the miscarriage. They had her lie down and put her legs up on the wall. Delia, Joaquín's cousin, rubbed raw eggs over Michelle's abdomen. They prayed, both in Spanish and Q'eqchi'. The next day, her body expelled the fetus.

We were afraid. We were not alone in that fear. Father Clarence and the others in the Maryknoll house—I don't know their roads, don't know how they "handled" Dianna's kidnapping and torture after it was over. I don't doubt there was that can-do Catholic missionary streak in them, *Get back to work.* That's what Michelle did. She threw herself into prepping for the Saturday meetings and spent more time visiting barrios. That was her way; it still is. She learned to smile again. People asked about her health. She assured them she was fine. Others said, "It will happen. You'll have children." Only then did she falter slightly, but changed the conversation to something more alegre, more life-giving. Joyful.

I didn't, not for a while. The abduction, the soldiers surrounding the house, and the miscarriage shook through me. Insomnia came on, which roused the mood swings. It was difficult to leave the house. An old tic came back into play, one created in childhood, when the relative took me, when I would look to the upper corner of the room to try to escape: I jerked my head to the right, two, three times in a row. I started doing it again in Guatemala. It still happens, whenever childhood rushes me or the disease takes control. Now, any stress that becomes too much brings on the tic.

Chapter 23

The women who had helped Michelle during her miscarriage showed up at our door one morning with a baby. Delia held the boy in her arms. She said, "We thought you'd want to take care of him, until they find his father."

A farmer, on his way to his corn crop, had come across the foundling, wrapped tightly in blankets and lying on the edge of the path. Later they learned that his mother, who was near death and delirious with amoebic dysentery, had left the baby there and wandered off. Her husband was in a crop that was far away from Poptún. He spent his nights there to tend to the corn. They had sent word about what happened, but it would take days for him to find his wife and return.

Delia said, "Since you just lost your baby, we thought . . ." She trailed off, as though not needing to explain the rest of it. I balked. This was not a good idea. It had only been two weeks since the miscarriage. I stuttered half-baked reasons but didn't get too many words out before Michelle took the baby from Delia and forgot about the world.

Just like that, she became a mother. A mother who ignored all sense of logic. She had fallen in love with the baby the moment he was in her arms. A baby that, the women reassured us, would be with us only a couple of days, before the father returned. There was no talking sense into Michelle, though I tried, saying, in so many words, that we shouldn't get too attached. She ignored me, and kept cooing at the baby.

We crowded into the kitchen, where the women stood around Michelle and the child like loving sentinels. She sat at the supper table and talked to the boy as though he were her own. No, not *as though*. In that instant, Guatemalan child and gringa missioner became one.

I asked Delia, "What's his name?"

"I don't know. But they say his father's name is Lázaro."

"Then we can call him Lazarito."

Little Lazarus. Michelle liked that. She put him to her shoulder as though to burp him, and whispered the name in his ear.

He was three months old but weighed less than ten pounds. His arms looked like lean pieces of wood that splintered into kindling fingers. His eyes were slightly sunken in their sockets.

I had my doubts; but soon, it also rose in me. It had come on before the miscarriages, but with Lazarito, it hit me hard. I wanted a child. I wanted to do fatherhood right.

Two days later, around four in the morning, Lazarito woke and started crying. Michelle, half asleep, said it was my turn. His diaper needed changing. Forty-eight hours previously I couldn't even approach him when it was time to do this. Now, I dexterously unwrapped him, lifted his legs, cleaned, and ducked my head so he didn't pee on me. After some Desitin cream smeared on his butt, I rewrapped him with a clean diaper. He looked up with those large, walnut eyes. I fed him a bottle, put him back in the makeshift crib of thick blankets stuffed into a large washing tub, and returned to bed. I lay awake until dawn but didn't mind, though I knew the day would be wrecked for lack of sleep. Before Michelle woke, I got up and stood at the washing tub. I leaned in to hear his breathing—such calm, tranquil breaths—then kissed his forehead.

Then I jumped. This wasn't safe, not for the heart. He soon would be gone, once they found the father. I scolded myself, *Don't get attached. He's not ours.*

The father had yet to arrive. For three more days our lives circled around the boy. We took him to the clinic for a checkup. Neighbors chipped in and collected a pile of baby clothes. When we walked the streets, children and mothers gathered around us, googly-eyed over Lazarito. Which I didn't call him at first. I continued to call him "the baby." In refusing to say the name, I lied to myself, and believed the lie.

I asked Delia when the father would return. She had heard he'd be back in a few days, that he was tending to his wife in a clinic in Flores, the capital of the Petén, which was far north of us. Delia must have seen the worry in me, and said, "He's coming. It's his only child." Of course, of course. Soon, we would hand little Lazarus back to his family.

Many in our barrio thought differently. They used the word *regalar* often in conversation, to give as a gift—adoption. "Maybe Lázaro will give him to you all. They're so poor, they'd want the best for him."

"No, no," I said, "he needs to be with his family." Yet they had planted the idea deeply into our hearts. It was coming on more and more, the notion of fatherhood, and the promise to do it right.

Another day passed. Lázaro still hadn't arrived. The very hours turned against Michelle and me. Each time we changed a diaper and fed Lazarito a bottle, a ghostly umbilical cord wrapped around the both of us, attaching us to him.

Delia knew something had to be done. "I found out where they're from," she told me. She mentioned a village, whose name I don't remember, which was about a two-hour drive away. We made the decision: Delia would go with me to the village, as she knew the way. She spoke Q'eqchi' and could explain to the villagers why a gringo was walking into their midst with one of their own in his arms.

Michelle said her goodbye, kissed him on the forehead three times while muttering to him in Spanish and English, then handed him over to me. She turned away before I could get out the door. I heard my wife wail for the first time in our lives together, a woman whose motherhood had been taken from her twice in one season.

Delia and I drove to the village. She sat in the passenger seat, holding the baby, while I dodged holes and stones on the road. She pointed to a small path in the woods. "That's the way in," she said. I parked. She handed me Lazarito and took the two bags filled with diapers, formula, medicine, clothes, and bottles. I carried the sleeping babe.

A woman came out of the jungle, with a bundle of firewood balanced on her head. She and Delia spoke in Q'eqchi'. I saw it on the woman's face, the shock that the lost child had been found. She had us follow her. I cradled the boy tightly to protect him from a muddy fall. After another twenty minutes of walking through the woods, we stood in the center of a bunch of *champas*—huts made out of thin reeds and straw roofs. All eyes fell upon us. They gathered around, children, mothers, a few men. They offered me a seat. Only a few spoke Spanish. Delia translated for me. "He has thrush on his tongue," I said, and showed them a vial. "He's very malnourished, here are some vitamin drops." We talked about feeding him. One woman said that a neighbor was breastfeeding her own child and had enough milk for three more. My heart leapt at that. I knew that breast milk could save his life.

We chatted for a while. Soon it was time to go. Too much tumbled out of my mouth. He had been with us for a week, but he was no bother at all. "You see, we have no children, and my wife, she was more than happy to take care of him, he brought her a lot of joy—" I stopped myself, handed him over to the nursing woman, and said, "But it's good he's home."

They thanked me for my services and wished me well. No chance of regalar. Today was not the day for gifting a child.

"Goodbye, Lazarito," I said, uttering his name for the first time.

He looked up at me with those walnut eyes. It was too much. I wished the villagers well, then walked away, passing Delia, who rushed her own goodbyes and followed me.

All of this could have been avoided a week previous with a quick, "No, I'm sorry, we can't take a child in right now." That would have made sense. That would have been logical, to recognize that the motherly hormones that had risen in Michelle just a few weeks previous were still running in her body, her mind. *It was a mistake*, I thought, yet now I know it wasn't. The heart has its own logic.

I returned to a silent house. Michelle and I shared some whiskey before going to bed. We awoke to old schedules, making coffee, cleaning up the house, preparing for work. We followed known patterns, without Lazarito screaming at us for attention, without the responsibility of dirty diapers and boiling milk bottles. We returned to our places, to a certain emptiness. But the longing had been planted in us both.

Chapter 24

As I think back to those years in Guatemala, it feels as though both my illnesses—manic depression and PTSD—dried up, which is not true, at all. There were constant battles with insomnia. I drank to fall asleep. I was moody, as I'd always been. But I wasn't having any flare-ups that I can remember, no sudden outbursts. There was too much going on, outside of my mind, that kept us on alert.

Life was becoming ominous. The special forces Kaibiles didn't stay in their training camp, but started roaming the streets, along with the foot soldiers. They wore red berets and camouflage uniforms. It was easy to distinguish them: the foot soldiers would, when they were bored, start to slouch, and smoke, and gather together to pass the day walking the streets. The Kaibiles did not slouch. They were straight as pins, and muscular, with eyes that revealed a training that was beyond what a regular soldier received.

They rarely looked us in the eye, but when they did, a fear would pulse through us. When a Kaibil walked by, a person might cross the street to avoid his gaze. We knew they trained not just for war; sometimes they dressed as civilians and drove white pickup trucks through town. It was no secret that the Kaibiles also made up the death squads that roamed about at night. People knew to stay indoors whenever a truck passed.

Our meetings at the church became more subdued, with fewer people attending. Chamba told us that it was time to pull back on the land distribution talk and turn to teaching the sacraments and Bible study.

We followed his advice. Confirmation time was coming up, when teenagers make the choice to follow the teachings of the Catholic Church for the rest of their lives. We met in the chapel. They sat in the pews and I stood before them, just in front of the altar. I had chosen Exodus as the theme for the day. I was on a roll: Moses's birth, his adoption by the pharaoh's wife, his inevitable return to his Jewish roots, and his radical acts against the ruler with the outcry *Let my people go!*

In the middle of my lecture, a Kaibil walked into the church. He did not genuflect, as though to say, *I am greater than God*. He stared at me all the way to the pew, where he sat, right in the middle of the teenagers, a girl to his left, a boy to his right. They stiffened but did not dare look at him.

I froze up inside and became acutely aware of what I was teaching. There's no getting around the fact that Exodus is about an oppressed people struggling for their liberation. I was going to softly connect the story with our times, just a little wink of a reference to Guatemala's own history of oppression. Looking back, I see how stupid that was. But I was in my mid-twenties and still believed in a certain sense of invulnerability, until the Kaibil walked into the church.

He was a decorated man, perhaps a lieutenant. He stared at me for a full twenty minutes as I talked, trying my best to soften the story of Moses, avoiding the liberation part. Then, as if having heard enough, he stood and walked out. At the door, he gave me a last, hard gaze.

After the class I ran to the parish house and looked for Chamba. He was taking the afternoon off, swinging in a hammock that hung in an open hut. A beer stood on a wooden chair to one side. He smiled at me. "Marquitos," he said, using the diminutive for *Marcos*. "How's it going?"

The moment I mentioned the Kaibil, his smile dropped. He sat up in the hammock and listened to the whole story before saying, "They do that. Just to make you shit your pants. Sometimes they record you. But more than anything, they're telling you who's in charge. What was it you were teaching?"

"Exodus. The flight from Egypt."

He looked at me as though I were an idiot. "I said to stick to safer subjects. And you go and pick Exodus." He shook his head. "Why didn't you go all the way and say that Moses was a communist?" His anger was hiding his fear. "Pull back," he said, then said it again, harder.

I went home. Michelle and I talked about it. She said what Chamba had said, that we had to be more careful these days. I didn't sleep that night, nor the next. It was coming on; but I had no breakdown, just a fit of nerves that stayed with me all through the days. I looked at my wife with a certain awe and jealousy—just like in Nicaragua, she was handling things, seemingly better than I was. This pissed me off, her ability to forge on the way she did. For it had been I who had broken down after Nicaragua, I who had feared rabies from a well. Michelle had returned to the States without a scratch of PTSD in her. I felt weak before her, and I resented that as well. What had happened in Nicaragua, I swore, wasn't going to happen in Guatemala.

But the invulnerable shell I had constructed around me was cracking. No longer was I looking for mine fields to walk in. There wasn't any need to walk toward any danger; the danger was following us all.

*

I buried myself in my writings. I was working on another novel, one set in a small jungle town in Guatemala. Though I had not sold any book, I wrote as though on a deadline, spending four hours in the morning at the kitchen table, writing out the story in longhand on yellow notepads before rewriting it with a typewriter. It helped to calm me, as writing had always done. If I missed a morning due to lack of sleep, or because of the Saturday classes, the anger would start to bubble, along with a panic that seemed to come from nowhere.

I dug more into a daily routine: write in the mornings, do calisthenics afterwards, visit people in the afternoons, attend religious services in the barrios, and finish the day off with a couple of shots of whiskey.

One day around noon, Michelle visited a nearby village named Machaquilá, where they were celebrating their feast day, one of the holidays for the blessed virgin Mary. I couldn't go, as I had a scripture class to teach in one of the barrios. We preferred never to travel alone, but Machaquilá wasn't that far away, and it was full day. She took the Jeep out of town and made her way to the village.

On the outskirts of town, soldiers stopped her. There was one Kaibil amongst them. He stood to the side, watching. Other cars before her had to stop to have their papers checked, then the soldiers waved them on. Michelle handed one soldier her registration and license. He glanced at the papers, then stared at her. She didn't move. He let her pass. She geared into first and took the dusty, rocky road to the village.

At the end of the celebration, Michelle stood up with a few

announcements from the parish. She asked if anyone needed a ride into Poptún to do some shopping or run errands. No one did. She said her goodbyes and drove off, alone.

The soldiers stood at their little post to the side of the road. They were still stopping cars. Michelle thought that since they had checked her just a couple of hours earlier, they would wave her through.

A small car slowed down ahead of her. This time it was the Kaibil who was checking papers. When he spotted Michelle's Jeep, he waved the car on, as though disinterested. Then he stopped Michelle.

There were no vehicles behind her. The little car had driven away. No buildings, no houses. Only the countryside, her Jeep, and the soldiers. The Kaibil stood next to her and said, "Let's see your papers."

"I just showed them to you hardly two hours ago," Michelle said. She reached for the glove compartment. Four soldiers walked around the Jeep. They surrounded it, one in the front, two on the passenger side, one in the back. They pointed their M16s straight at the Jeep. The Kaibil opened her door and said, "Give us a ride into town."

She froze. The Kaibil started to cajole her, saying, again, that they could take a ride together, but now didn't mention town, just the ride. One of the soldiers on the passenger side tapped on the window and grinned. Michelle looked at him then turned back to the Kaibil. She blurted out, "I'm sorry, but I work for the Catholic Church, and my bishop forbids us to give rides to anyone with guns."

That was a warning to them: After Sister Dianna Ortiz's abduction, the Guatemalan military, due to international pressure, had backed off from church workers.

The Kaibil growled at her, calling her so many names before his voice rose in a shout, "¡Ah la gran chingada!" He slammed the door, told the other soldiers to back away, and yelled at her to drive the fuck off.

I was home when she arrived. She fell on her knees. She couldn't control her sobs. I held her for a long time, it seemed like all day and into the night. I was frightened, scared shitless. But I was also amazed at how quickly she had thought in the moment, using her position as a Catholic missioner to make the soldiers back off. She had talked herself out of a possible kidnapping. When I think on it, I still look at her with awe.

Chapter 25

They had placed the girl on a cement bench just outside the hospital. Joaquín Che' Ax and I arrived with a pine coffin, one he had hammered together that morning. Along with gardening, Joaquín was also a carpenter, and in the past few weeks he had been busy making coffins. Cholera had swept through the jungle towns of Guatemala, killing people by the hundreds. The hospital didn't cure anybody. It was more a waiting room for the dying.

The inside of the ramshackle clinic smelled of vomit and shit. The sick were laid out, one next to another, on beds, foldable cots, rugs on the hallway floors. Once someone died, the orderlies carried the body outside to the waiting families, while more victims of the disease stumbled through the front door.

The dead girl on the bench had no family waiting for her. Joaquín and I stood in their stead. Two orderlies had carried her out on a stained stretcher. One of them apologized for leaving her on the bench, but said there was no room inside to keep the cadavers.

She might have been five or six years old. The slab she lay on, the unpolished, concrete, backless bench, was cool to the touch. She was still warm. She was dressed in the indigenous clothing of her people: a dark red blouse with tiny embroidered flowers around the neckline, and a wrap-around skirt woven out of the green, blue, and white threads of the Q'eqchi'. Her clothes were not stained. I figured the cholera had emptied her out in her home, and someone had dressed her before bringing her to the hospital. No doubt the fever had finally killed her.

Joaquín and I placed the coffin beside the bench. I stood and looked at her before putting her in it. It wasn't my first dead body, though the others had all been babies, most who died before their first birthday from worms, amoebic dysentery, or some strange fever that had its roots in poverty. Not that I was inured to handling deceased babies; but it had become one of my religious tasks, a service to the families of the dead. And I wanted the job, though it took years to figure out why.

I dug my left arm under her shoulder blades and slipped my right hand under her thighs. She was warm and felt alive for it, but her one loose arm fell and dropped to her side. I had to hoist her from the bench and jostle her to balance her weight in my arms. Her head slipped off my shoulder and fell, pulling tight the dark brown skin under her jaw. I adjusted her again to take her out of that awful position. Her head fell onto my shoulder. Her face was right next to mine, her lips close to my ear. The movement unkinked her throat. Her mouth was open. Trapped air in her lungs slipped one last time over her larynx. She whispered *Aaaahhhh* to me.

The mother arrived. She carried two clear plastic sacks of insulin that she had bought at the pharmacy, as the doctors had instructed her to do. She was young, maybe nineteen, and was dressed just like the girl. She didn't speak Spanish. She stared at her daughter in my arms, dropped the insulin bags, yelled in Q'eqchi', then rushed to my side. I crouched and laid the girl in the coffin, straightened her head, which rolled to one side, crossed her arms over her chest, pressed her legs together, and tucked her dress under her calves, working like a clumsy mortician. Her mother knelt next to the coffin and caressed the girl's face. Joaquín gave her a moment, then gently spoke to her in Q'eqchi' while pulling her away. When we placed the lid and Joaquín started hammering, the young woman raised her head and cried out as though hating the heavens.

Michelle was working in another part of town. I sent word to her that we needed the Jeep to take the child and mother back to their village. She arrived ten minutes later, parked close to the coffin and opened the back hatch. She comforted the mother, put her arm around her while the woman wept and howled.

Joaquín and I loaded the coffin into the vehicle. It didn't fit. We had to leave the hatch open. That was a worry. The pockmarked, stony roads could chuck the casket out of the Jeep.

Joaquín left to check on the sick inside the hospital, I suppose to take a preliminary body count to build more coffins.

I opened the passenger door for the mother. She hesitated, looked at me as though deciding whether or not to trust me, then looked at the vehicle and its interior, all of it strange to her. But she was too broken to argue, and climbed in. In between sobs she said the name of her village, a hamlet near Machaquilá. Michelle drove us out of town.

Nearly a third of the coffin stuck out through the open hatch. The roads made it impossible for Michelle to drive smoothly. I had to press my forearms against the head of the box to keep it from falling out. All those preparative acts of faith—the crossing of the arms over her chest, straightening her head, tucking her dress—had been a waste of time. She rolled inside. Her head bashed against the pinewood walls.

There were no soldiers at the roadblock. The hamlet was far beyond Machaquilá. We crawled over the jungle road for nearly an hour before reaching it. Night came on. We crested a hill. The coffin slipped a few inches. I hugged it. The headlights slashed across the hamlet's thatched roofs and stick walls.

The people stepped out of the flickering shadows of their champas, away from the few candles that burned inside the huts, and into the violent slash of the headlights. An older woman saw the coffin sticking out of the back and yelled something in Q'eqchi'. One young man walked out from behind a hut, his lithe arms to his sides like a man with invisible holsters on his hips. The father. I wondered why he hadn't been at the hospital. He had his machete still tied to his belt-rope. He had probably worked all day in a rich man's fields, clearing the land for cattle.

His wife, sitting in the passenger seat, cried out his name, "¡Cux! ¡Ay, Cux!" She was trapped inside a metal box, that's what the Jeep was to her, a thing she had rarely seen before, much less ridden in. The car door made no sense. She hurled herself against the vault of steel and vinyl. She beat her palms against the glass and screamed. Michelle reached over and grabbed the handle. The mother tumbled out and fell to her knees. She crawled to her husband. He picked her up and held her, while others gathered around them. An old man and a teenage boy hauled the box out from under me. They didn't look at me, as though I wasn't there. No hello. No customary, Mayan humble greeting. They pulled her out and didn't close the hatch, and carried her into the black jungle where the headlights couldn't reach. The entire hamlet followed, each of them disappearing into the night, leaving us alone before their empty, thatched homes.

Michelle and I had seen, during our time in Central America, what the statisticians refer to as a high infant mortality rate. But the stats show only numbers. They cannot reveal what that rate does to a people, how it forms within them certain beliefs, superstitions, and tricks of psychological survival. Many parents we worked with did not name their babies until two seasons had passed. To do so meant becoming too attached. Not naming the baby was a psychological ruse, *Don't get too close*. It never worked.

We had participated in babies' funerals before. I remember one nameless child, perhaps nine months old, whom I put into a rush-job of a box, its corners uneven, with a few bent nails on the edges. Joaquín hadn't built it; someone in the family had. They stood around me. The mother, between sobs, cursed herself for rousing the wrath of God. She confessed to having thought about what name to give the child in recent weeks. She couldn't help herself. She had considered names, ones that she had never uttered. But God, she cried out, had heard her thoughts and was punishing her for them. Having the baby die was the Lord's way of putting things straight. She said all this while I placed the child in the box, atop a folded blanket.

In the cemetery, they asked me to say a prayer. I asked God to bless the innocent soul of . . . and I had to stop. No name. The mother dared to evoke God's wrath once again, "I meant to name him Javier, after his grandfather." *I*. Her taking sole ownership of naming the child surprised me. It felt like a threat: Anyone who dared to shush her for saying the name, or who came down from Heaven to give her a smack across the face, would have to deal with her.

I had stumbled into the job of handling the dead. I was driven to do it, a macabre notion to some. Not to me. I wanted to hold dead children in my arms, to cradle them as though they were alive. This was when my own past bled into our days in Guatemala. It was as though what the relative had done to me in childhood killed off a part of me. Sometimes I see the incest rape as a deceased child floating around in my body, festering. I want to hold him; I want to raise him from the dead.

For three nights after we took the girl to her hamlet, I didn't sleep. It was coming on. But the insomnia made sense. I had held a dead child in my arms, had delivered her to her community. She had breathed on me.

I cut back on coffee and used more whiskey to get to sleep. I wondered what was going on, why my rhythm was so out of whack, as though not recognizing that the world we lived in was not a stable one, at all. As the Kaibiles wandered the streets, the fear rose in town. Something was changing for the worse and everyone knew it. They spoke of it in whispers and quick conversations. They also became accustomed to the changes, as though they had a choice. *This is the way it is. This is our life.* They had no other life waiting for them anywhere, unlike us, who could leave the country at any time. But we didn't leave; we didn't want to. This was home. We planned to be in Poptún for the long haul. And someone was coming around the corner, one who would solidify the commitment to stay.

Chapter 26

We would name her Raquel. It would take three months for the adoption to be complete, months in which her mother, Esperanza Rodriguez, could have changed her mind and taken Raquel back. But she didn't. Esperanza wasn't Mayan, but mestiza, a mix of Spanish and indigenous heritages. She might have been in her mid-thirties. She was from the forgotten world, the poorest of the poor. A woman with children but no man nor community in her life. No home, no one to support her. She drifted from town to town, looking for work wherever she could, washing clothes for a family, digging beans for a farmer, working in the corn crops. Anything to get by, to feed her two surviving children, Maura and Carlos, eight and four years old.

Hers was a dangerous world. She was exposed to the elements and to malicious men. She and the kids had slept in barns and in woodlands. Once they reached Poptún, she found an abandoned shack on the outskirts of town.

We would never know what drove her into such poverty. Nor would we learn about the father. Had she been raped? Had she gotten with a man for protection, until the man abandoned her after leaving her pregnant? I can only imagine the suffering she had gone through. Suffering that brought her to make perhaps the hardest, most painful decision of her life. But she had been resolute about it. She had once had five children, but three had died of malnutrition. In Poptún she had visited the town doctor, a man named Morales, and told him straight out that she was pregnant, and that she didn't want this one to die like the others. She had chosen to regalar.

The doctor didn't pin her down on who the father was, or why he wasn't with her. He said he knew a gringo couple who were trying to have children, but couldn't. *A gringo couple.* I wonder how Esperanza responded to that. Maybe hope—gringos were rich. But gringos were strangers in their midst; could we be trusted? I don't know what she thought. What I do know, from our conversations with her, was that she was *decidida*, committed to giving her child away for the babe's own sake, even though it tore her insides out to do so.

Twelve hours after Esperanza gave birth, Raquel was in our arms. The adoption would take three months of paperwork, which a Guatemalan nun named Sister Cheny, who was also a lawyer, filed. We sweated through those months, while also falling in love with someone whom I was afraid at first to call my daughter. We talked objectively about the process, how Esperanza could take Raquel away at any time during the months of filing. That was her right. All this while feeding Raquel bottled milk and changing her diapers and cleaning burp-vomit off my shoulder. We would not get as close as we had to Lazarito; we couldn't stand another heartbreak like that. All foolish notions. We were in love with Raquel the moment we put our eyes on her. I knew that if Esperanza decided to take Raquel back, it would tear Michelle to shreds.

But Esperanza didn't. Three months passed. Sister Cheny had all the papers ready to sign. We were waiting in the parish kitchen. Esperanza sat in the front den with Cheny. This was the way Cheny wanted it: to explain to Esperanza, alone, the entire set of papers. This took time. We sat in the kitchen, petrified. The cook took Raquel into a back room, where she cared for her while we waited.

Finally, Sister Cheny came in and sat with us at the table. She didn't speak for a moment. This was it: Esperanza had changed her mind. "No, no," Sister Cheny said, "but she wants to talk with you before she signs."

We went into the den. Esperanza smiled, but she was nervous. The four of us sat around a small table. Cheny had the papers before her. She looked to Esperanza and nodded her head. Esperanza looked at her, then at the table, then at me, straight at me. She had just one question. She said that people talked, and some had warned her what could happen to a Guatemalan baby in gringo hands. She asked, "I just want to make sure, when you go back to your country, will you sell her?"

This didn't surprise us. There had been scandals before, of foreigners coming into third world countries to steal babies and put them on the open market. I don't know how widespread it was, but it was enough for people to question.

Oh God no, we would never do that, we want Raquel, we'll take care of her, she'll live a good life. Then I said, as a light joke, "Don't worry, Doña Esperanza, I won't let her leave our home until she's thirty."

It wasn't a joke to her. She seemed relieved. Sister Cheny took the papers and spread them out. She showed Esperanza where to sign and reminded her, one final time, that she had the choice. My body—I couldn't tell if the others saw it quake. Michelle didn't move.

Esperanza thanked Cheny. She said she had made up her mind, and she put her X on each paper.

I can still see her, shaking our hands, thanking us, emphasizing how much she was happy *that you're going to take care of her all her life*. She walked out the front door.

The last I heard about her, she and her kids had found a home with an older man who had a small farm far into the mountains. He needed help around the house and on his land. I like to believe that she found a permanent home with him, and that he treated her kindly. But I don't know.

Raquel was beautiful, brown, and, as the months passed, fat. People called her *la cachetona*, the big-cheeked child. She smiled a lot and, by the time she was six months old, had a hearty little laugh about her. She became our life. We took her everywhere. At the Saturday meetings, we placed her in a wicker basket filled with blankets. We didn't get as much work done, not with the women passing her around. We took her to the barrios whenever making home visits. If there were any rancor in the air about gringos coming in to take one of their own, we didn't hear it, not among the folks we worked with. I think us adopting, then staying in the country, helped. We hadn't come to Guatemala to get a child and run back home. We were neighbors, church workers; we had made friends.

Raquel brought us deeper into the community. We as a couple made more sense now—for we were old, twenty-seven, and, in the minds of our friends, should have had kids ten years before. "Now you're complete," Delia said to us.

Raquel anchored me. I couldn't articulate it at the time, but felt it—I had a new purpose. I was a father. Something was welling up in me. *Get your act together* seemed to be the message. Along with *I want to do it right; I want to be a good dad*. I knew there was something screwy about my racing thoughts, insomnia, and bouts of depression. I had to deal with that. Raquel gave me that focus, which was good, for she was born in the worst of times.

*

Joaquín Che' Ax, who worked with us in the church meetings, was also our gardener. We didn't have a garden out back, but lived on the edge of the always-encroaching jungle. His job was to take a machete to the tough plants and vines that seemed to grow overnight. He cut a path through the brush and briars from our back door to the outside latrine. It was a weekly job, but sometimes I wondered if he should come back every day, to keep the jungle from swallowing the house whole.

He had suffered a slight stroke a few months before, which kept him at home for a while. He lost some of his speech, but he could still handle a machete. After so many weeks of bedrest, he decided it was time to get back to work.

I worried about this, considering his sickness. But he started cutting back people's' jungle-lawns again. In the marketplace, Michelle saw María, who said that Joaquín would get to our house on Thursday.

Thursday came, but he didn't show up. That was strange; he was never late, and usually came a little earlier to beat the heat. A couple of hours passed. I figured something might have come up at his home. Or maybe he had gotten sick again.

I walked to the Che' Ax home. María smiled and greeted me. I asked about her husband. "Joaquín's not home yet," she said, "he's still got a few gardens to cut back."

I told her that he hadn't shown up at my house. She thought that odd. "You're the first house of his day."

She had two grandsons who were around ten years old. She told them to run to the other homes where Joaquín worked. They did and within the hour returned. Joaquín hadn't shown up at anyone's house.

We searched the town all afternoon. No one had seen him. It dragged on into evening. I drove from barrio to barrio with one of María's grandsons with me. No luck. It was getting dark. We regrouped at María's house. Michelle was there; Raquel was asleep in her arms.

We had covered every barrio. We knew that the only place left to search was on the roads that surrounded the town, the dirt roads with no streetlights, only jungle. I drove out of Poptún with the grandson, who didn't talk; he was too busy studying wherever the Jeep's lights beamed.

We drove slowly on the back roads for over an hour, then returned to María's house. He hadn't come home. We stood in their small front yard and talked about what to do. No need to go to any authorities. The few police in town were an apathetic group who wouldn't worry themselves over a missing "indio." María was desperate. "Maybe I should talk to the one in charge at the military camp. They might know something." Then she thought better of it.

Raquel had woken up and was getting cranky. I took her home, while Michelle stayed with María. An hour later Michelle rushed through our door. "They found him," she said.

Someone had come to the Che' Ax home, a man whose name I don't remember. He had given María the news, "They've taken him to the hospital." María had peppered him with questions too fast for him to answer: Was he all right? Had he fallen and broken a bone? The man just stood there. María got quiet. She put one hand to her mouth. Underneath it, she whispered prayers. Finally, the man said that Joaquín had died, and they were holding him at the hospital until someone from the family came.

María barely caught her breath. "How did it happen?"

"They killed him."

Everyone knew who *they* were.

We drove María to the hospital. The doctor said that only two people could enter the room where they had Joaquín. María asked for me to go in with her.

He had his workday clothes on—old jeans, scuffed boots, a well-worn, short-sleeve button-down shirt. The bullet wound was in the middle of the shirt, right in his sternum. Then there were the bruises on his arms. I walked closer. María stood behind me. Joaquín's hands were to his sides and laying on the slab. Those were rope burns around his wrists.

I turned to María. She was stone. I figured it was shock. Doctor

Morales came in. He was about to pull a sheet over Joaquín. "No," María said. She didn't explain why. She walked out of the room and told one of her grandsons to go get a new set of her husband's clothes, and also to tell Delia, Joaquín's cousin, to come to the hospital. Michelle drove the boy home. About twenty minutes later they returned with a clean shirt, Sunday dress pants, underwear, socks, shoes, and Delia. María whispered to Delia, asking her something. Delia nodded. María left. Delia turned to me with the clothes in her arms and said, "Will you help me dress him?"

It took time. He was a small man, and thin, but it was still clumsy, turning him left then right on the slab to pull his shirt off. I peeled his pants off him. Delia got the shirt completely off. There was the hole. I turned away. Delia called for an orderly to bring her a bowl with soap and water in it, along with a wash cloth. She cleaned the wound. For a moment I thought about evidence, that we were destroying it. A foolish notion. There would be no investigation. The next day we buried him.

María spoke little in the days following. She spoke less to us than before, even though Michelle and I visited her every afternoon. It was fear, of course. We all feared, because we all thought it. Had they killed Joaquín because of his involvement in our work? Or was he just a victim of a cadre of Kaibiles who decided that beating and killing a man would be good fun? Was he simply another victim among the thousands upon thousands of Mayans who the dictatorship had had killed in the name of anticommunism?

We spoke in low voices about it. María did talk, but it was more of a mumble. I couldn't understand her ways of mourning. Stalwart. Demanding. And as far as I can remember, she didn't shed a tear, at least not in front of us. I wondered if it was a form of acquiescence to the world we lived in: A Kaibil camp on the edge of the town. Soldiers all through the streets. This was their lot in life. This was their reality, one they couldn't escape from. María, I believed, was giving into this. As though she had a choice. The following weekend she didn't attend the Saturday morning class, nor the next.

*

A few weeks later, Michelle and I woke up early to prepare for the adult education class. At seven she answered a knock at the door. It was Carole

DeVine, Mike DeVine's wife and the owner of the bed and breakfast on the edge of town. She stared at Michelle as though seeing nothing, and muttered, "Mike's dead, they killed him last night."

Carole's arms trembled as she reached toward a chair. She told us what she had learned: At three in the afternoon the previous day, Mike was driving his van from town back to the farm. According to a farmer who was in a nearby crop, a white Toyota with no license plates, which had been parked there for hours, had forced him to stop. One of four men got in the van with Mike. Both vehicles pulled away. He never returned home.

Mike's workers searched for him. They found the van off the road in the shade of some trees, with the keys still in the ignition. Mike lay behind the van. His hands were tied together. He had been decapitated.

Carole asked Michelle to stay with her. I ran around town with workers from the finca, trying to get hold of a coffin big enough to hold his corpse. I also was the one who verified the body in the clinic.

Doctor Morales stood on the opposite side of the slab, the same slab they had placed Joaquín on. "I did my best," he said, like a man apologizing. "I sewed it up completely." He pointed directly to the line of black crisscrosses over the pulled skin of Mike's neck. "You wouldn't know it was severed if you couldn't see the string."

On Sunday, most of Poptún showed up at the cemetery. Mike had been a well-liked man, a quiet, shy, gringo *patrón* who apparently never got involved in anything controversial, or political, or any other words the military used to rationalize their right to murder.

After his death, the town shut down. We spoke of the murder in whispers. Again, for a while, fewer people showed up to our meetings. It was on everyone's minds—they had killed a gringo. It meant no one was safe.

They never fully understood why a death squad had murdered Mike. There were rumors. Supposedly the military, which was involved in the international drug trade, running Colombian coke through Guatemala on the way to the States, had asked (or ordered) Mike to use his bed and breakfast as a stopping point along the way. Mike refused. According to someone who was nearby, the colonel had said to Mike, "Fine. But you should put your affairs in order."

His death created an international furor. A gringo had been murdered. There would be an investigation. But no clear theory came from it. I've seen papers from the CIA through the Freedom of Information Act. Most all the papers are covered in black. There are hardly any words to go on, just short sentences that tell you nothing. His death is still a mystery, like Joaquín's death. Some things are never known.

*

No longer was I contemplating death by my own hand. I wasn't the same man who had walked into a mine field in some deliberate act of martyrdom/suicide. I was afraid, like everyone else. Both of us were. Michelle and I rarely left each other's side. We never went out at night; nobody did. It was all about staying alive. My past didn't prick at me as much as it once had. It was as though the violence around us temporarily put the violence of my own childhood at bay.

We would stay in Guatemala for another year after Raquel's birth. In memory, that year seems quieter. I wonder if the Guatemalan military had seen that, in killing a gringo, they had gone too far in the eyes of the international community. I don't know. But according to my journals, we got back to work. The people returned to the Saturday meetings once more.

One Hundred Years of Solitude was still with me. I didn't carry it around in a backpack anymore, but kept it on my desk. Its spine was starting to crack. Some pages fell out of it when I picked it up. But I read it again while in Guatemala, at the desk, carefully flipping the pages. The more we lived there, the more the book spoke to me, made sense to me. For one, I started to see that the book is not linear at all, but a circle, an encapsulated century that repeats itself, much like the Mayan concept of time.

This time I read it like a teacher preparing for class. I took prolific notes in my journal—mostly a synopsis of events, a way of putting them in order so as to remember the various story lines. Even the incest, or the constant warnings against it throughout the book, until it finally happens, didn't put me in a bad place, because I saw something in it that made complete sense to me: The incest in the novel comes out of solitude, and that solitude is the demise of the fictitious town of Macondo. Incest destroys, not only the people involved, but the community itself.

We were in our late twenties, and I was still in that *Fuck the past I live for now* attitude that had served me well throughout my life. But that sense of invulnerability was getting chewed away. I was a father now. Another's life depended on us. Raquel roused in me teachings that I had learned in seminary, about being a good man. I wanted to be a good father. I had several examples to follow: The Hansons, who had taken me in during my junior and senior years of high school. The Tanners, who were good to me, even while knowing I was a depressed, suicidal teenager. And Michelle's family, who ate together every night, all eight of them, around a crowded table that my mother-in-law covered with nightly homemade suppers. My father-in-law asked each of his children about their days, basketball games, upcoming exams, a boyfriend whom he hadn't met yet. Her parents were involved in their children's lives. I wanted to be that way.

The thicker Raquel got (she was one hefty child), the more focused I felt. Fatherhood set in deep. I don't remember being too overprotective. It didn't bother me, but pleased me, to see Raquel in our coworkers' arms, to watch Father Chamba kitchy-coo her in Q'eqchi' and lift her over his head. Women made over her, men would hold her on their laps while we taught classes. They treated her with the same love that my Villatoro family in San Francisco had given me. I wasn't afraid of others holding our child, and I now believe it was because we were living in the antithesis of solitude, in a community that I trusted. And that community helped to make her the happy, giggly baby that she was.

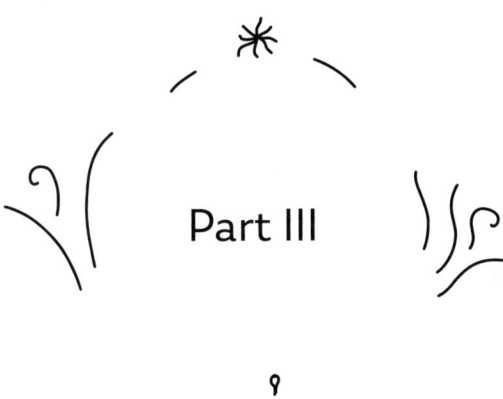

Part III

Chapter 27

Our lives in Guatemala ended abruptly. Soon after Raquel's first birthday, we made a trip to Iowa to attend the wedding of one of Michelle's sisters. Michelle started throwing up and craving strange foods. We met with a doctor. He told us straight out that because of her previous miscarriages, she could have another one and, if she wanted to do everything she could to keep this baby, she needed to stay put.

It's a shred of memories: Michelle never got to say goodbye to Poptún. I had to return to pack up all our belongings. I videotaped people who sent blessings to Michelle, many who wept but who also were so happy for her pregnancy. Delia prayed it would all turn out well and that Raquel would soon have a baby brother or sister.

María looked into the camera. She had changed since her husband Joaquín's murder. No longer the bubbly woman who served tamales at the Saturday morning classes, she had fallen into a deep depression. Yet, when she spoke over the videotape to Michelle about the pregnancy, she managed a smile.

Father Chamba was disappointed. He said that our work had really gotten off the ground, even during the violence, and that more people were becoming involved. But on the video, he gave a loving farewell in all three of his languages: Spanish, Q'achiquel, and Q'eqchi', then threw in a little English, "We will miss you."

*

I returned to the States, which was a world away from what we had just left. It pricked at me. I wanted to be back in Guatemala. So did Michelle; it hurt her to watch the videos of people saying goodbye. We had seriously considered taking the risk of flying back to Guatemala, but the doctor only had to give us a straight look to show us how irresponsible that would be. He was right, of course; to suffer a third miscarriage could be crushing. But Michelle's belly grew big. She had Emily Jean in March of 1992. Raquel didn't care at all for that at first, but ended up cuddling with her little sister for photos.

We were a happy family. I was going to turn thirty soon. Children make us vulnerable; I was losing my macho-man attitude. I had built a wall of invulnerable manhood to protect me from the past, but I needed to bring down that wall, the one I had propped up all my life. Actually, I had no choice; the wall would fall on its own.

But it didn't fall immediately. There was too much to do. We had two children. I had to find a job. It was as though too much was going on for me to have a nervous breakdown. I didn't suffer the PTSD that I had upon our departure from Nicaragua, which surprises me still, as Guatemala had been so violent. Not that I was calm. There was a constant tremor of anxiety in those first few months back in the States. But that made sense. We had been wrenched out of Guatemala, which weighed on us both. We hadn't wanted to leave; we had been happy there. The work had purpose: the adult education classes, visiting the sick, helping with Father Chamba's land-buying project. We had lived a Guatemalan lifestyle, going to the open market every other day, where we made friends with the merchants. We had had a life there. And I had delved, as deeply as possible, into my Latin American roots, not realizing that those roots were helping me deal with my own past.

Michelle and I ached to live in a Latino world. But we were once again in the US South; where would we find it? I searched for jobs and discovered a program that was also all about social justice. An organization called Glenmary wanted to become involved with the growing population of migrant farm workers in the southern states. That's why they hired us. That's how we ended up in Alabama, where Mexicans picked acres of tomatoes, worked on tobacco farms, and slaughtered chickens in the Tyson poultry factory. It was a world within a world: over three thousand Mexican workers had made their way into the state and had clustered in one area about an hour north of Birmingham. They became our new community.

*

In Los Angeles, where we now live, I buy my drinking water from the "Watería" store in my neighborhood. Rosa runs the place. We speak in Spanish, mostly about our kids. It's a friendly relationship. But one day she launched into a story about a man who had come in the day before. He had been belligerent and coarse, and had flung curse words at her. She said, "Of course, the guy was Salvadoran."

I figured that Rosa was Mexican. I let her go on for a while about the savagery of Salvadoran ways before telling her that I too was Salvadoran. I smiled when I said it, to take the sting out of the words.

Her jaw dropped. She said that I didn't look Salvadoran. She was vexed. "You're such a gentleman, how can you be Salvadoran?" I told her my father was white. "Ah," she said, "so *that's* where the goodness comes from!"

It's not everyone, of course, but there is an animosity between many Salvadorans and Mexicans. The anger goes back a long, long way, though I haven't met a Salvadoran or Mexican who knows when it began. It's our own Hatfield and McCoy story: one doesn't trust the other, but they don't know why. It's just the way things are.

One theory is that it began in 1821, shortly after Central America gained its independence from Spain. Mexico tried to swallow the region into its empire. The fiercest opposition? El Salvador. They went to war. Eventually, Mexico left El Salvador and the other Central Americas alone. But the bitterness remained.

More recent events haven't helped. Due to the wars in the 1980s and 90s, thousands of Central Americans had fled their countries and made their way to the United States. They had to pass through Mexico. Such a huge population of refugees crossing the border made for more cultural clashes. Today, Salvadorans flee the gang violence in their country. They crowd the border between the United States and Mexico, hoping for asylum. I can only imagine the tension between the two peoples, one rooted in the far past.

As a kid, I didn't know anything about this hatred. There were no Mexicans around for my mother to react to. She never mentioned it. When we went to Mexico to spend the winter holidays with my Uncle Paco, I didn't feel it. Mexico had opened my eyes. I was completely ignorant of the fight between the two cultures and only learned of the feud when we moved to Alabama.

Alabama, of all places. Oneonta was the name of the town, one smaller than my hometown of Rogersville. There was one grocery store—the Piggly Wiggly—an elementary and high school, a diner, numerous Protestant and Evangelical churches, a hardware store, feed store, and one street light. Not a liquor store in sight. I'd guess the population to be around a couple thousand in the town, with a dozen farms surrounding it. Not exactly a multicultural town—the African American population was small. But it became multicultural quickly once the Mexican migrant farm workers started showing up to pick tomatoes.

The change in the demographics happened in the usual manner. Single men came to the United States looking for work, and even though they were paid shit for picking tomatoes, it was more than they had made in the Old Countries. They came in, worked the crops, and went back home. The next year, they'd bring their wives and, the year following, dared to cross the border with their children. Once the families got more-or-less established in trailer parks and ramshackle houses, they brought in the grandmothers—and once you've got grandmothers around to take care of the kids while you're bending over tomato plants, you're starting to put down roots.

In memory, it happened quickly: one minute we were in the jungles of Guatemala, the next, in the plateaus of northern Alabama. It's a jolt of recollection, a rattle of actions that had a specific goal in mind: to settle down. We now had children. I knew that meant we wouldn't return to Latin America, not in the near future, maybe never. I mourned that. But in Alabama, we could continue to live in a Latino world. My plan was to shove myself into the Mexican community so deeply, I'd forget I was back in the States. That wasn't about to happen, at least not in the first year. Had she been around, my friend Rosa at the Watería in Los Angeles could have warned me about that.

It wasn't until we bought our home just on the outskirts of Oneonta and had paid about half a year's worth of mortgage payments, when my subconscious started to say, *Okay—time to get to work on yourself.* It was a quieter life. Our children were growing. Raquel was three, Emily, one. We were settling down. The quietude gave my mind a space to relax. At first, I didn't struggle so much with racing thoughts.

Now, in Alabama, in the peacefulness of a small, old house that sat on five acres of woodland, with a pond, and deer that would wander through our front yard in autumn, I could shed the Mighty Me. As if I had wanted to, as though it had been my choice. But this would be different than the asylum that had been Wesley Woods in the Smoky Mountains. In Alabama, it was in the peace of a middle-class life, where the demon rose. The one demon, which set off the other.

*

It was difficult to do organizing work in a migrant community, mostly because, by the time we got some organizing done, Immigration came through, rounded up a few dozen people, and sent them back to Mexico. Every few months, large, dark blue, windowless vans would come through the area and round up every Mexican they could find. They usually hit the trailer park on the west end of town, which had filled mostly with migrant workers. It was a futile endeavor; they couldn't whittle down the Mexican population. Men who'd been taken in those vans from Oneonta and had been tossed onto the south side of the Texas-Mexican border, would just cross the border once again, make their way back to northern Alabama, and get back to working the fields.

Our friend Chepe Gonzalez, a man in his mid-thirties who had been working in Oneonta for a few years before we arrived, and who had his entire family living in a small house in the middle of a tomato crop, had been picked up by *La migra* several times. He just laughed about it. "They send me home. I spend a few days with family, eat my mother's food, drink with my friends, then cross the border again. It's like a vacation."

Chepe was all swagger. He was a chain smoker, a drinker, and known to be one of the hardest workers in the area. A good-looking guy, with what my mother would have called "bedroom eyes." He didn't just pick tomatoes, but drove the trucks that carried the cargo to warehouses in Birmingham. He had a really good fake driver's license. Cops figured he had papers. He didn't. Most of the people we worked with had no green cards or residency documents.

Chepe may have acted flippant about the INS raids, but they worried him. It was more than a disruption. Sometimes parents would be taken from their children and sent off to Mexico. We hid people in our home while the vans drove through town.

Our work was more about advocacy than organizing. Michelle became an interpreter. She spent a lot of time in the clinic, translating between a doctor and his Mexican patient. She met with local pastors who wanted to do outreach to the Latino community but weren't sure how. And she learned the ins and outs of the bureaucracy of immigration documents for people who were applying for residency. She made a lot of trips with families to Atlanta, where the INS had their regional offices. She wasn't popular with local lawyers who had found a new source of income from desperate Mexicans who needed to get their papers, most of whom paid in cash.

It was in Alabama where I learned that migrant farm workers were also financial wizards. Somehow, with the pittance they got for working in the tomato fields and the Tyson chicken slaughterhouse, they not only paid their rent and food and upkeep for their vehicles, they also sent portions of their salaries home to Mexico. They worked hard and impressed their farm bosses, many of whom didn't hesitate to make comparisons. "I get more sweat out of these Mexicans than I do any white trash or nigger around here," a farmer once said to me.

It was a strange world, with whites, African Americans, and Mexicans all living in the same county. Even with Alabama's history of being one of the most racist states in the nation, there was little animosity shown between the cultures. At least not overtly. Our Mexican friends did grouse about their bosses every so often. But there was also a strange form of friendship that you'd sometimes find between employer and employee, though the Alabamians always had the upper hand, paying their workers far less than they had to pay a US citizen. No animosity, just some moments of friction from time to time. That's what I thought when we first arrived.

*

It was Chepe who first pointed out our differences. "Your Spanish, it's . . . not like ours." He pointed out my use of the word *vos* instead of *tú*. "You must have picked that up from living so long in . . . where'd you say you lived?"

"Nicaragua. And Guatemala."

"Oh. So that's where it comes from." He nodded, as though saying, *That's all right*. I told him my mother was from El Salvador. His eyes widened. He took a drag from his cigarette. "You're fucking kidding me. You don't look it." I told him about my father. "Oh. So that's why," and made a circular gesture to my face. He laughed and added, "Don't tell anybody you've got Salvadoran blood. They might send you packing."

But word got around. Others started to kid around with me, especially during parties, where the whiskey flowed. We'd gather in someone's trailer and have a good old time eating posole and pig-brain tacos and downing Wild Turkey. They'd joke with me more harshly than I was used to. I started to see the differences between my Salvadoran heritage and the local Mexicans'. They were, in my mind, rougher than the people we'd worked with in Central America. This made sense. They were farmers to the bone, had lived tough lives, had crossed borders and into states that hated them the moment they saw them coming. Many of them cursed like my father, just in Spanish, which taught me more words that I tried to take on: *pinche, chingado, vergazo*. But they didn't feel right coming out of my mouth. *Pendejo* was one word we all owned, universal throughout much of Latin America. But they didn't understand my Salvadoran idioms and I didn't comprehend their Mexican sayings. Sometimes I had a hard time keeping up with their conversations, especially when we drank. They'd get on a roll about the back-breaking work of stooping over tomatoes and chopping off chicken heads. They'd talk about a fellow whose thumb was cut off by a rolling blade at Tyson's, and how the company didn't do shit to take care of him, because they didn't cover health insurance for undocumented workers. That's when the anger would raise its head, when the injustices were laid out on the table between the shot glasses, pinto beans, and piles of white tortillas. The shit pay. The INS. The white people in town who didn't like them at all, and who were the ones who called Immigration from time to time to "clean out all us 'Spics.'" They'd argue about African Americans, some of them parroting what their bosses said about them being lazy, while others said that the whites were as lazy as the blacks, and another would clarify, "Of course they won't do our jobs. They're Americans. They expect to get paid real salaries, and not the fucking coins the jefes pay us."

This all felt like great opportunities to tap into their anger and rouse some organizing work. But their lives were too unstable. Though they had planted roots here, they also knew how easily those roots could be torn out of the earth, with just one phone call to the INS from a disgruntled local. I suggested that we bring the community together to talk about these issues, and do something about them. I had no idea what that something would be; I figured ideas would rise from the group. Some agreed. Others said that any type of organizing would just rouse trouble.

I didn't push it. But they started to push—against me. They got on me about having guanaco blood, first jokingly, but it started to turn acrid. I was three drinks into a party, and was starting to get angry the more they talked shit about Salvadorans. At one point I said something, I'm not sure what, but it was a tepid riposte.

They laughed. It was my friend Chepe who said it. When he drank, he could get mean. I still remember his words, "Tú no eres Salvadoreño. No eres nada sino un pinche güero." It stung like a thousand bees: *You're not Salvadoran. You're nothing more than a fucking white boy.*

All those years in Central America, all those years of finding my Latino roots and clinging to them as a form of salvation, and with just four words, Chepe sliced me to the bone. *You fucking white boy.* I figured then that I'd never really be a part of the Mexican community. I'd never be invited into their midst, as I had felt while living in Central America. In fact, Michelle was more accepted than I. They treated her with a certain deference. They saw Michelle in the courtrooms, where a sorrowful man who'd been caught drinking and driving would depend on her to translate him out of the predicament. She stood with pregnant women in the local clinic and made sure they got fair treatment. When it came to advocacy work, she was fearless, even when talking with immigration officials. It was that fist-on-the-hips, can-do, Iowa-German, Liberation Theology–trained attitude of hers that got things done. She didn't hesitate to say to a doctor, "It doesn't matter whether or not Mrs. García has papers, by law, she's got as much right as the next woman to prenatal care." Then she'd turn to Mrs. García and, in a gentle Spanish, promise her that she'd be getting a checkup soon, which she did.

But I wasn't an outcast. Considering their precarious lives, most of the migrants were thankful for anyone who worked as their advocates. We weren't the only ones helping them. Many white folks from Oneonta reached out to the new community. One Baptist church offered free child care in the summertime for the mothers and fathers who worked in the fields. Though my own faith had been waning since the days of leaving the seminary, I had to recognize how the Alabamians' religious beliefs drew them closer to the people who were doing all the work in the tomato crops and the chicken processing plant. Jesus was calling them to help. They sent school buses into the trailer parks and countryside roads, early in the mornings, picking up migrant children to bring them to the parish, teach them English, feed them, and, for most of the day, let them play. They took care of the babies and toddlers, giving them formula milk and pureed carrots, which they paid for out of their own church funds. This was a great help to the migrant families, who could never afford child care. The Baptist church had run the program for three years by the time we moved there. The migrant farmers, especially the mothers and grandmothers who worked with their husbands in the fields, were very appreciative of this service, until the day came when all hell broke loose and sent a shock wave through white and Mexican communities both. A day that would finally break me.

Chapter 28

My hometown of Rogersville is about a four-hour drive from Oneonta. My parents visited us from time to time. Both of them had retired. They were able to, because my mother pulled the same magic trick that our Mexican friends did. As much as they had struggled, Mamá had budgeted so tightly, she managed to pay off their mortgage in twenty-three years on a thirty-year loan. They were both in their seventies. They had settled, somewhat. The anger still flared from time to time, but they didn't have the same energy to keep the flames stoked. And now, they had grandchildren: two granddaughters and a third baby on the way. Our son José David was born in Birmingham about a year after we had arrived. My parents visited more often.

It was strange, to watch my father with my kids. And I did watch him, closely. Though I was never sure whether or not he had had anything to do with what the relative had done to me, I didn't want him to be alone with them. But after a long while of vigilance, I saw that he, an old man, wasn't about to hurt his grandchildren in any way. He doted on them. Once he brought a large, pink ceramic piggy bank with him, along with two pants-pockets worth of change, and taught the girls how to slip the quarters and dimes into the slot. He sat on the carpeted floor with them, while Raquel and Emily dropped the money, mostly to hear the *clink* of the coins against the ceramic. "Now that's how you save up your money," he said, "by gosh, I'll make skinflints out of you yet!"

By gosh. He rarely cursed around them. Oh, he'd slip up from time to time, such as when he'd lie on the couch and raise up one of the kids over his head and sing, "*Tell me a story, tell me a story, tell me a story remember what you said!*—ah goddammit, what's the rest of the words . . . ?" I didn't know; the man hadn't sung one song to me in my own childhood. Where the hell did this one come from?

My mother's doting on them wasn't a surprise, as I had experienced enough of that when I was a boy. But Dad just didn't make sense. It pissed me off, of course, the way he loved his grandchildren, the way he was soft with them. Whenever he rolled himself a cigarette, Raquel and Emily would watch with fascination. He'd tell stories about a flying squirrel that he'd shot out of the sky, or catching a fish so big that it wouldn't fit in the trunk of the car. He never raised his voice. Whenever the two sisters got in a little spat, such as over a dollar bill that Dad had dropped onto the pile of coins, he'd say to one of them, "Now honey, no need to fight, here you go," and hand over another dollar.

We took trips to Tennessee as well, though I found it more and more difficult to enter my parents' house. It felt like a haunting. The kids stayed in the room where I had slept as a child, and still I didn't make the connection.

Our children roused certain teachings that I had learned through the years. I remember Father Murphy from seminary, who once had quoted from the gospel of John, *Our sins will be on our children and their children's children.* We were talking psychology at the time—how abuse, alcoholism, neglect, and all the other dysfunctions within a brittle family can pass from one generation to the next. "But it doesn't have to be that way," Father Murphy had said, "the chain can be broken." I see the wisdom in that now, because I know that yes, it can happen. We can, if we set our lives to it, break chains. I want to explain to my younger me that the house in Tennessee haunted him, for good reason. But my children ran through that house with no haints, no fears of being attacked. In memory, I see a sheen, the same mist that had separated me from the refugees in the Nicaraguan camp: on one side of the curtain are my children, running around in my parents' front yard. On this side, I am in that room in the far back of the house.

In Oneonta, we had a home, steady jobs, meaningful work. We lived in a Mexican world that, while occasionally kicking my ass for being a *güero-guanaco*, also welcomed us into their community the longer we lived there. No violence, no threats of encroaching battles in the mountainsides. We were settled. We were parents. A certain peace had come into our lives, a peace that created a safe place for the inner violence that had been planted in me in childhood to come forth.

I was squirming. Or, better said, it was squirming in me. The insomnia was coming on again. I drank whiskey at night after Michelle and I tucked the kids into bed. I feared night itself *when it happened*, something I couldn't make sense of at the time. All I knew was, the evenings now scared me. *Why am I feeling this way? There's nothing going on!* It made no sense. It wouldn't make sense until something out there revealed to me what was going on inside. Something that I had seen before, and had touched, with a strange, dark longing.

It was, by all accounts, an accident, though the Mexican community wouldn't see it that way.

The Baptist church's school buses had made their rounds throughout the county that blistering hot July day, picking up the children of the migrant workers, to take them to the day care they had set up at the parish's school. The buses were filled to capacity, with children who spoke both Spanish and English to one another while the driver took them to the church. They ranged in age from toddlers to middle schoolers. There was one baby on board one of the buses. She was around six months old.

The day care center had gotten so busy, they had to bring in more volunteers. Michelle and I helped out from time to time. I became a puppeteer, using our children's stuffed animals as props. Suddenly, Mufasa, from "The Lion King," could speak Spanish. Michelle taught the older kids the basics of drawings and watercolors. Our daughters played with the other children, while women cuddled our newborn son, passing José David to one another so everyone had their turn.

We weren't there the day it happened. We heard about it through Chepe, that a baby had died on the Baptists' watch. That morning, when they had emptied out the school bus, they'd overlooked the child, whose name was Carlita. She had been strapped into a car seat. The kids had run out of the bus, and the volunteers had shepherded them to their classrooms. Carlita must have been asleep when the bus driver locked the door. Alabama summers are brutal. By ten o'clock, the temperature had reached ninety-five degrees. The day care center was at its maximum capacity. In all the bedlam, no one noticed Carlita was missing until two hours later.

Her death ripped open the seam of a hidden rage within the Mexican community. It all came out, beginning with Carlita's family, who lived in the trailer park. Here they were, in a foreign country, doing the work no gringo would ever touch, having to dodge La Migra whenever anyone took the notion to call the authorities, and living in the dilapidated trailers in town and the shacks out in the tomato fields. They used the words we had heard all throughout our time in Latin America—poverty, injustice, oppression— and added on from their own experiences of living here: The racism against them, the shit pay and the jefes who weren't always so easygoing with their workers, who kept them in the fields longer than they ought, who made them work double-shifts in the chicken plant, and who themselves threatened them with Immigration if anyone got out of hand. And Carlita. How could anyone leave a baby on board of a baking bus? Wasn't anyone watching? Wasn't anyone checking the seats to make sure all the children got out? *No, because they hate us. They use us, then get rid of us whenever we ask for a little more pay, whenever we bring up work conditions at the chicken plant, the accidents that happen when we work overtime, worn to the bone from chopping up chickens for twelve hours straight. They hate us and don't really care, even when they kill one of our babies.*

People gathered in the trailer park, where they prayed for the soul of little Carlita, and prayed for the family, and prayed for them all. They asked Michelle and me to be with them and wanted me to lead them in a rosary in their trailer. I got on my knees with over a dozen people, most of them women, with the men standing outside the trailer, listening, their heads down. I was well-practiced with the rosary and, though I didn't believe the words, followed the ritual with the solemnity of a monk. I said the first part of the Hail Marys and the people responded with the second half, like the refrain of a song. Afterwards, Carlita's mother, Alejandra, turned to me, called me Don Marcos, and said, "They killed my girl." She didn't weep. They had been discussing it. Others in the family whispered to one another. Alejandra said, "I want you to find out if they meant to."

All this happened within the day. At first, the local clinic wouldn't let the family see the body, which just added to the community's suspicions. Alejandra said to me, "They'll let you in." I wanted to say that it wasn't necessary. I wanted to say that it was an accident, that no one would want to kill a baby in such a way, and that the Baptists were having to deal with the police now, who were investigating the death. But I didn't. I knew better. My choice was a simple one: I was their advocate. I did what they asked.

Alejandra said to me, "Check her for wounds. Check every inch of her body."

She was right about the hospital. The doctors let me in. But I wasn't alone; Chepe was at my side. There was fat little Carlita, on a soft mattress atop a slab. They had covered her with a small blanket. I took it off. She still wore the clothes her mother had dressed her in that morning, a light blue dress and tiny white shoes.

I lifted Carlita gingerly from the mattress, as though she were still alive. She was cold, as cold as the air-conditioned room. Chepe watched. Alejandra had said, "If you have to, take her clothes off." I couldn't do that. I cradled her head in my palm and checked her skull for contusions. There weren't any. I checked her neck for cuts. Nothing. I turned her one way, unbuttoned the dress just enough to see her tiny back, buttoned it back up, looked at her legs, took off her shoes and socks and studied her feet.

Chepe said it before I did. "It was an accident." But he was angry. "Those fuckers should have been more careful."

The doctor verified that Carlita had died from heat stroke, but Alejandra wasn't about to believe that. She waited until my report. Once I told her, and Chepe backed me up, Alejandra and her family and the neighbors turned quiet. But the anger still simmered. Soon Alejandra left with her two surviving children. They returned to Mexico.

There was no revolt, as many a local Alabamian feared. In fact, their fear seemed to come from a hidden place, as though they believed, all along, that the Mexicans, those good, passive people, could turn on them in a second. Nothing happened, no Mexican uprising, and no retaliation from the locals. The world got back to the way it was, with foreigners doing the work that no one from here would touch. Michelle returned to helping people with their papers and translating for them in the clinic, the police station, the courts. Still, there was tension in the air, and it lingered a long time.

*

Something was happening. I started to close down. I was going inward, without want. I stayed home more, didn't venture out with Michelle as much. I wanted to be with our kids, all the time. José David, who was about the same age as Carlita, was alive, *so alive, look at him kick, listen to him cry, watch him roll over.* Our daughters ran about the house, played with toys, flipped through picture books, and walked with me around the pond, tossing small stones into the water. We were a settled family, healthy, alive. But something had died in me—no. Something had been dead all along.

My fear of the nights was growing. I was afraid I'd never sleep again. Then there was something else—what was it? A vague thing, something that slipped through the invisible mist, approaching me. Vague but familiar, though I acted as if I'd never seen it before. I hadn't, not in this way, not in this moment that happens again, it always happens again when I write about it, when I focus on it for a second too long.

The past was pressing out from inside, against my flesh, as though to burst it open. I considered helping; I considered the old pocketknife, just a small cut, to let the pressure out. But I didn't. There were children in the house. There was my wife, who noticed the changes but wasn't sure what to think of them. I was more than moody. The erratic fear shook me like a rabid dog ripping apart a rabbit. Whenever sleep did come on, I sometimes bolted up from the bed in a night sweat and looked around the bedroom, at the window, where the light from a slivered moon was too much.

I relied more on daily order: writing in the morning, jogging through the countryside at noon, taking care of the kids when Michelle went to work. Our children were growing. Michelle was pregnant again. Life, new life. I craved it, desperately so. *Live. Live. Live to the fullest.* For there was so much life around us, especially in the house, with three kids keeping the place loud and raucous. All was well. I said that to myself, *Everything's all right, there's nothing going on, so why do I feel this? Where is it coming from?* It felt like mania, but not in the same way as the ebullience of the past. It morphed into something I had not felt before: someone was out to get me. I felt like I was always looking over one shoulder then the other, to catch the attacker coming from behind.

It was building, like gas in an enclosed room. All those dead children. I see now why I touched them, picked them up, placed them in coffins, checked them for wounds. I was cradling the dead child in me, holding it as though to resurrect it.

But life in Alabama showed another truth. There were living children who scattered their toys throughout the house. They were not I. They were my son and daughters who sat on my lap and gave me slobbery kisses. They yelled, they cried, they laughed. They needed me; I needed them. And I watched Michelle, who balanced her days with work and motherhood. She sometimes took the children with her. Our kids made friends with Chepe's children and were learning as much Spanish as they did English. Michelle celebrated their birthdays with cakes made from scratch, and she decorated them with ornate scenes from every Disney movie we watched. No one made a better piñata than she. Our children were everything to her. She celebrated their very lives in a way I had never seen before.

I was their storyteller, and I taught them Spanish songs. I showed them the dances my mother had taught me, and I spoke to them in both languages. Sometimes the girls stood on chairs and watched as I made tortillas for supper. I sang Spanish lullabies to them at bedtime. It was all good. It was beautiful.

But the tremor was still in me. I desperately followed my daily schedule to keep order in my head, a semblance of normalcy, which wasn't working. I remember the day it happened, remember that in the morning, I was trying to get baby food down my son's throat, who just spat it right back at me. Then he smiled, a real, honest-to-goodness shit-eating smile. So alive. So, untouched.

The day passed. Night came on. The family went to bed. I drank but did not sleep. I paced through the house and walked between the corners of all the rooms, in a pattern that made no sense: walk to one corner then the next, and the next and the next, then go to another room and do the same. I checked on the children all night. I stood over my wife, whose soft breaths rose in the air like peace. The dawn came. Michelle found me in the bathroom, as though someone had shoved me like crumpled paper between the tub and the toilet. "Honey? What's the matter?" She rushed to me, pulled me halfway out of the cubbyhole and held me while I screamed, over and again, *He raped me he raped me he raped me.*

Chapter 29

That breakdown in the bathroom with my wife was the beginning of a type of healing. I had screamed as though the trauma had, at age thirty, occurred to me for the first time. In a way, it had. I had pushed it down for so long, in an act of self-protection. I had distracted my mind, knowing that the abuse was always there, but pretending it had no bearing on my life. Yes, it was a form of denial, a specifically manly one, macho, daredevil. One can hold that pose only for so long, before the past erupts out of your earth and swallows you. In Alabama, in the peace of a home in the woods, with children encircling us, and with meaningful work, it was as though my mind had said to me, as it had said to me when I first heard the *Adagio for Strings* in college, *You can fall apart now. This is a safe place, to lay that burden down.*

I did lay it down. But not silently. I spoke about it with others, friends whom I could trust with the story. The retelling eased the pain somewhat, though there was always shame involved, as though I had played a role in my own suffering. As though it had been my fault. It would take a few years to discover therapy, where I could speak freely with a professional, let all my emotions out without the irrational fear of repercussions.

But back then, I had no psychologist. All I had was my voice, one that, after the initial horror of full recognition of what had happened to me, turned into rage. I was, and am, thankful for that.

*

The relative had kept in touch with my parents through the years. I had rarely spoken with him. Soon after we had returned from Guatemala, and before we moved to Alabama, he had contacted me with a small job proposal. He worked in video, making training films for companies' new employees. One company needed a Spanish translation.

We had needed the money. I took the job and translated the script. He had also wanted me to narrate the video. But he got busy with another project and had to put the Spanish film to the side for a while. By then we had moved to Alabama. He called a few months after I had faced the truth of what he had done. It was, in retrospect, perfect timing.

He started to get testy over the phone. He said it was time to record the translation. I said I couldn't, that my job took up all my time. We argued, but not for long. It was as though my whole body was on fire. Then he said the thing that unleashed the flames: "You owe me."

Just the right thing to say. I flared.

"I owe you NOTHING!" And it went from there. I ripped him apart on the phone, and, to put a real sting to it, cursed him out in both English and Spanish. It didn't take long—he backed off like a tick from a lit match head, apologizing, and saying *Oh God, oh God*, as though he had dreaded this day coming. *I'm sorry, I won't bother you again, you don't have to do the job.* I didn't let up. *You fucked me as a kid! You raped me!* He apologized over and over again, but it was too much for him. He hung up. I breathed like a wild beast that has bolted across a field and torn apart its prey.

After five years of working with the migrant farm community, I was accepted into the Iowa Writers' Workshop and had just signed a contract for my first book. We were planning to leave Alabama. With a fourth child on the way, Michelle wanted to be a stay-at-home mother. In Guatemala, during the adult education classes, I had found my love for teaching. My hope was to get a job at a college somewhere, anywhere. It was time for a change.

Before we left the South for the last time, we visited my parents. The house in Tennessee haunted me more than ever. I slept on the couch in the front room. I couldn't wait to get out, to move to Iowa, to escape.

My mother was not in a good mood. I remember her picking at me, asking me questions about things to do—what were those things? I don't know. All I remember is, she was harping about something. It might have been her own way of dealing with our departure. We were going far away again and, after Iowa, had no idea where we would end up. I'm sure she prayed that we'd return to the South, but she never said that. Instead, she went on and on about things I don't remember.

The house was becoming too much. Now, I was afraid to enter it. I needed to flee. But we were going to spend another night there, before driving to Iowa. I didn't think I was going to make it.

She asked me to take out the trash. Then she followed me outside and asked for something else. I took the aluminum garbage can and hurled it against the house. The lid snapped off. The garbage flew out. I had dented the can and left nicks in the wall.

Dad came around the corner. "Son? You all right?" He was old and had less meanness in him. "What's the matter?"

I turned on him. Both of them stood there. We were in a tight triangle. Michelle came out then rushed back into the house to tend to the kids, to make sure they didn't see or hear what was happening outside. I started to cry, but the anger pumped through me. Spit flew out of my mouth. I said, "He fucked me, over and over again, and you didn't stop it!" It went on a while, and they just stood there, listening to every word.

I bolted into the woods, the forest that I had played in as a kid. It was night, but there was enough of a moon to help me find the old trails, ones that hadn't been trod upon in decades. I stayed out there a long while. Michelle called out to me. I could hear her in the distance. But they must have talked, because she stopped, as though knowing I needed to escape.

I tromped through the forest and wept. Then I worried. I imagined Michelle calming the kids, telling them I was going to be okay, I just . . . I don't know how she explained it to them. What did my parents do? Did they talk? Did they sit in the room with Michelle and pretend nothing had happened? Did they worry about what would happen once I came out of the woods? Or, would I ever come out of the woods?

I did, after an hour of roaming through the forest. I didn't go in the house, but sat on a chair beside the barbecue grill, where my comic books had gone up in flames. A cloud must have covered the moonlight, because the night seemed darker than before.

Mamá came out. I couldn't see her face, just the shadow of her body. We didn't speak. My breath was erratic, but I was starting to calm down. Then she sighed and said, "Ay Marcos, lo siento mucho."

She continued to speak to me in Spanish. I don't remember all that she said. She didn't barrage me with explanations or excuses. In moments she turned quiet. Cicadas chirped in the trees. Then she spoke again, not about the abuse, but our future. Her voice was so soft. She said how wonderful it was that Iowa had accepted me, and that I'd get a good job after graduating. She would miss her grandchildren, but she promised that, wherever we ended up, she would make sure to visit every chance she could. Then a pause, and a tremulous sigh. She said, "Es mejor que te alejes de aquí."

Alejarse—to move, far away. That would be the best thing for me. The memory came on, from twenty years previous, when she had sent me away to high school. Through the years I had questioned that decision. Now, in the shadows next to the barbecue grill, I saw that she indeed had done it for my own good. She was doing it again. *Go away, far away from the source of the pain.*

She shuddered. This was, I knew, the beginning of her own nightmare. Pure regret. A mother who had failed to protect her beloved son. Dad, I'm not sure what he felt. All he had done after I had exploded was walk back into the house. But Mamá stayed with me. We sat out there a long while. Her Spanish was sinking into me. It felt like a balm. She ended it with words that she had said to me in childhood, whenever Dad wasn't around, when she would tenderly call for me to sit on her lap. "Ay mi cipote, te quiero tanto."

Sometimes that's all that can be said.

At times I've asked myself, had it not been for the abuse in childhood, would I have sought out so hungrily my Salvadoran roots? It's akin to the question: had the abuse not happened, would I not be so sick with bipolar? The latter I've no doubt of. The two illnesses—PTSD and manic depression—during times of duress, wrap tightly together. I cannot deal with one without also confronting the other.

Regarding my Salvadoran-ness, I don't know if I would have plunged into myself as I had, as I still do. The journey itself has not only kept me alive; it's defined me. I have defined myself. I know that there's still the Appalachian in me; it only took Chepe to remind me that I was a pinche güero to recognize this. I can't rip the Tennessee mountains completely out, and don't want to. It still leaks out of me from time to time, whenever I am speaking English. *Dang. Supper. You-all.* I don't mind that. It's a part of me. I love spending time in the Appalachian Mountains, though we don't get back there as often. Because of our years in Wesley Woods and living with the Mexican community in Alabama, I no longer throw the entire region out of my mind. It wasn't Appalachia that had hurt me. An individual had done it all, in a back room of a tainted house.

It's still a struggle, and it always will be. Sometimes the darkness comes on, as though I'm falling into a pit. I have to look at that darkness, and, in an act of pure will, try to put a space of objectivity between me and it. To say, "Okay, there it is. It's haunting me." It doesn't cure me, but it does allow me to function and, inevitably, work out of the horror, knowing that yes, the horror will come again, and knowing that yes, I can survive it.

But *survive* is a limited word. I want to do more than survive. The challenge is to get to survival and go beyond it—to thrive. To succeed. To love and be loved. This is an ongoing process. *La lucha sigue adelante.* The struggle goes on. *Vale la pena.* Of course it's worth it.

This story has been yet another barbaric yawp, another moment of telling the tale, one that I've told to anyone who can withstand hearing it. For we must be heard. We must cry out, in whatever languages we have, against the malevolent. We must nurse our wounds. We who have suffered under the hands of others, must take out full vengeance on those who had set out to crush us: we must scream. We must *live*.

speak of it

Epilogue

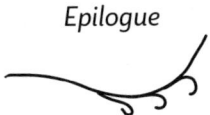

In Los Angeles, there is a small plaza in my barrio that always smells like Central America. The roasting meat inside one of the shops mixes with the *mazeca*—wafts of tortillas, tamales, chuco, pupusas, all things corn. Latin American music constantly blasts through its windows. Sometimes, while on a walk, I like to stop and stand in the parking lot in front of the restaurant, just to take in all the odors, the sounds, the Spanish. Here, on the corner of Victory Boulevard and Kester Avenue, I find my Central American home.

Home is everywhere here. We live in Van Nuys in the San Fernando Valley, where a huge part of the population is Central American. It's a working-class neighborhood, with pawn shops, second-hand stores, and bail bond offices. It's also a place of pupuserías, Latin clothing stores, and Spanish. We've been here twenty-four years. We raised our four children here, who are now all adults and living their own lives.

Before moving to Van Nuys, the two years in Iowa were difficult, not due to the studies, which I loved, but for the abundance of frozen-hard snow and the lack of any Latinos. After living so many years in Latin American worlds, the time in Iowa felt empty, lonely. I learned a great deal about writing poetry and prose there, and I made friends with a few of my classmates. But it wasn't enough. It lacked the culture that fed me.

After graduating from the workshop, I got a teaching job at Mount Saint Mary's University in Los Angeles. Michelle works as an art teacher in a high school. Eighty percent of the university's student body is Latino (at Michelle's school, it's ninety-five). Most all of them come from struggling families from Watts, Compton, East Los Angeles. Mine are mostly first-generation college students. Many were born in Mexico, El Salvador, Guatemala, Honduras, Nicaragua. Others were, like me, born here. Some feel directly connected to their heritage. Others feel the separation, that of having been raised in "Gringolandia." Through the years, I've met students who are caught between both worlds and who are looking for a return to their Latino roots. Improving their Spanish is a main goal. I help them with that, talking with them as they stumble through the words. I see now that there are many like me, people who yearn to find their own cultures. It is for them, in great part, that I have written this book.

I also tell the story as a way to fight against the stigma surrounding both mental illness and abuse, to open the door for others who suffer, and to teach people not to keep such suffering to themselves. But it's hard to tell the tale. Afterwards, I fall into a slump of sudden depression, self-loathing, and doubt. I fear authority—someone, due to my telling, is out to get me. The relative will somehow attack once again. It's all irrational, or course, except in the mind of the survivor.

Then it passes and, when the time is appropriate, I tell the story again. But this is the first time I've put it to paper. I wrote this in sections, small scenes that at times overwhelmed me. I had to put the manuscript away for weeks at a time, before returning to it to write the next part. I took breaks and turned to the one book that has helped keep me grounded for four decades. During the spaces between writing, I pulled *Cien años de soledad* out of the shelf and thumbed through its pages, reading sections out loud, just to remember the story and to keep my tongue trained. Now, after finishing these last words, I plan to spend several quiet mornings reading through that fiftieth anniversary edition, without a pencil or dictionary, just myself and the text. It will be yet another journey into the roots of who I am, who I have chosen to be.

Gabriel García Márquez, in one of his other novels, wrote something that has stuck with me since I first read it:

> La memoria del corazón elimina los malos recuerdos y magnifica los buenos, y que gracias a ese artificio logramos sobrellevar el pasado.

(The memory of the heart eliminates the bad and magnifies the good, and thanks to this artful device we are able to endure the past.)

I've wrestled with this passage. In times of illness, the bad memories are magnified and the good are seemingly snuffed out. But it is the *artful device* that brings me around to understanding—that device being the memory of the heart. My mind now doesn't just circle back into the traumatic past, but sweeps up the good. Those marble-playing, bat-killing children in El Salvador have been in my thoughts a lot, as have the train ride and the goat I vomited on. All good memories. They don't just counterbalance the bad. They remind me that the struggle to return to my Latino roots has been with me from the beginning. The struggle itself is a form of salvation.

I have suffered; and many, many people have been good to me all my life. They have shown me that the world is not all malevolent. They have taught me kindness, commitment, love, and the clamor for social justice.

All the tools that I have gathered throughout my life still help to carry me through the horrid times, when the illness comes on, when those diabolical days circle around me once more. And they will continue to circle. But so does my own journey into the Latino world, which has been there all along. The culture that cooed at me when I was a child, that held me in its arms and whispered, *Ay mi corazón, rey de mi vida*. I rely on those memories. I rely on my Salvadoran culture, the place where I was first loved.

Acknowledgments

I am deeply grateful to all the people who have walked with me on the journey to write this memoir. Every writer needs readers who are willing to delve into the work while it is still in progress. Michelle is my first reader. Her perspective was invaluable, as it helped me fill out many of the events in the book. Thomas Cook read and critiqued an early draft; his insights pointed me in the right direction. JoAnna Novak read the next-to-final draft and tightened it even more. Angela R. Morales and Eddie P. Gomez pored over the final draft and had great insight into its strengths and where it could be improved.

My agent and friend, Valerie Borchardt, is the final person to read my work before she sends it out into the world. She has the keenest eyes. She's critiqued all my books and they are the better for it. I treasure our *amistad*, a friendship that reaches back through the decades.

I thank my publisher Stephen Hull for not only accepting the memoir, but also for his own insights into the story. He and I have worked together before, on earlier books of mine. He's been a great friend to my writings, and to me.

A final shout-out to the organizations we joined in the 1980s and '90s: Witness for Peace, Maryknoll, and Glenmary. Michelle and I learned a great deal about social-justice issues through these three groups. Many of our cohorts were mentors who guided us through the work. In Guatemala, we were not the only missioners in the region; there were also nurses, priests, nuns, and lawyers, all committed to working with the poor and oppressed. For the sake of brevity, they did not make it into the book, but they left a lasting impression on us and changed our lives. I am deeply grateful that we had the privilege of working alongside them.

Excerpts of this book have been published in the *New York Times* ("A

Honeymoon on a Harley"), the *Wall Street Journal* ("The Demons in My Head Roam the Streets" and "The Mexican-Salvadoran Antagonism"), *Sequestrum Magazine* ("Getting Schooled"), *Tahoma Literary Review* ("Lost Hillbilly"), and *Pank Magazine* ("My Girl"). I've also written poems about many of the incidents, which have appeared in the *Pittsburgh Poetry Journal*, the *Bangalore Review*, the *Bookends Review*, the *Chicago Review*, and *Red Wheelbarrow*. A few scenes in chapters 7 and 8 originally appeared in altered form in my autobiographical novel *The Holy Spirit of My Uncle's Cojones*, published in 1999 by Arte Público Press.